The Export Gardener

Richard Harrison

CONTENTS

FOREWORD

When I was growing up in Melbourne, Mr Campbell would mow our lawns. I only really saw him during the school holidays, but how exciting it was to hear the faint rumble of his lawn mower in the front garden. That meant he would soon appear outside the sunroom windows, marching back and forth behind the silver birch tree. He was solidly built and deeply tanned, with powerful forearms that sported massive tufts of curly grey hair. I remember that he used to empty the grass clippings into big hessian sacks and how games of backyard cricket were all the more fun on a recently manicured surface.

CHAPTER 1

SOWING THE SEED

It was conceived as a great adventure. Live overseas for a few years and concentrate on what I had enjoyed doing most in my twenty year advertising career. I would work as a copywriter with an ad agency in the UK, while my wife furthered her legal career. Weekends would be spent editing my novel, travelling abroad and writing post cards home to the envy of family and friends.

That was the plan.

The reality became working as an office temp, commuting from South London, where I shared a flat with Catherine and her partner Deborah. Catherine was from Sheffield. She was pleasant, friendly and worked as a teaching consultant. Deborah was from Brazil. She spoke broken English and threw a decent left hook.

It was my by then ex-wife that alerted me to the Jim's Mowing opportunity. She was working in the franchise department of a leading UK law firm and dealing with a group of consultants who were in the process of establishing a platform for Jim's Group in the UK.

I knew of the business but nothing about it, before I was introduced to a fellow called Brian Duckett. Brian was the head of Horwath Franchising and he explained that Jim's needed someone to launch its business concept in the UK.

I thought it sounded like an exciting opportunity and we arranged to meet the following week in the foyer of the Novatel in Piccadilly. He drove from Oxford. I caught the bus in Streatham.

We sat down over tea and biscuits, all the while serenaded by a woman dressed in a ball gown and playing a harp. As you do when the conversation turns to lawn mowing.

Brian opened his laptop and proceeded to explain the structure of the Jim's franchise model. A concept that started with lawn mowing and had since spawned nearly thirty different divisions. He focused very much on its middle tier investment opportunity. Or at least I did. I could become what he called a Regional Franchisor, a role whereby I would secure exclusive rights to various Jim's divisions of my choice within a specific geographic area.

Thereafter, I would be free to operate my own business, while selling individual franchises to other people.

Mowing and (to a lesser extent) Dog Wash appealed and it certainly made sense to operate a franchise myself. Doing so would provide me with an income and generate a degree of awareness. It might also establish a measure of credibility, as I figured if I could do it, anyone could.

I had absolutely no interest in gardening, had barely mowed a handful of lawns in my life and couldn't tell a weed from a Wisteria. But hey, how hard could it be?

The 159 bus hadn't reached Brixton before my new business venture had been thoroughly mapped out.

There was no point staying in London. What I needed to do was live and work in the affluent stock broker belt that comprised much of Kent and Surrey.

The next day I hired a car in Croydon and drove more or less south out of London. Before long, I stumbled on the medieval market town of Sevenoaks in Kent. It had a quaint, particularly English feel about it and was clearly an expensive place to live, given it had several boutiques, countless hairdressers and a Ferrari dealership.

The town had no shortage of estate agents and over the next couple of weeks, I caught the train from London Bridge a few times to do the rounds. I only wanted a flat, but would need a garage to stow all of my equipment. The first agent I visited was Savills in the High Street, where 'lettings are handled upstairs.' I introduced myself to mid-thirties, suit and tie, and explained my circumstances, time frame and requirements.

'How much are you looking to spend?' he asked.

'Oh, I don't know,' I said, 'about five hundred a month.'

He looked at me as if I had just suggested he should marry his own sister.

'No good?' I asked meekly.

Clearly not. Apparently, a decent flat in Sevenoaks would set me back at least seven to eight hundred pounds a month. In any case, I didn't stay long, as 'we don't normally handle properties of that nature.'

It seemed those agents with a broad high street frontage concentrated more on the investment banker end of the market, with some even going so far as to adopt a 'no lettings' policy - a kind of real estate apartheid.

I did however manage to find a more suitable agent. 'Cavendish,' described itself as a 'lettings specialist.' It had an office in 'The Shambles,' a network of narrow lanes just off the High Street. My visit there was more productive, notwithstanding the fact I managed to twice hit my head on their 16th century ceiling.

I left with a copy of their listings for November and soon after booked a return flight to Melbourne to attend Regional Franchisor training at the Jim's Group head office in Mooroolbark.

CHAPTER 2

FOUR MEAT PIES AND A MARS BAR

'This is Jim,' the man said, explaining that I was the first UK pioneer, in Melbourne to attend the training course.

We shook hands and I told him that I was looking forward to moving out of London, working outside and writing a book.

'You'll be too busy,' he said.

I have no idea what the man is worth, but he owns Jim's Group, the world's biggest home services franchise. All the same he drives a 1981 Volvo, which has a coat hanger for an aerial, a chipped windscreen and one flat tyre. I am assured that on the rare occasions he travels interstate or overseas, he flies economy, catches a bus to and from the airport and stays in a backpacker hostel.

Every preconception that I had of the man was wrong. He was modest, unassuming, slightly built and short. What's more, unlike the bearded face that adorns every Jim's logo, he was clean shaven.

Soon after, I was introduced to Greg Puzzolo. He was in charge of the mowing division. A former franchisee himself, he was very enthusiastic and physically imposing. Tall, dark and heavy, he sported a thick bushy moustache and looked like Groucho Marx on steroids.

I had of course seen countless Jim's Mowing trailers on the streets of Melbourne and the business was clearly a huge success. It had worked throughout Australia, New Zealand and Canada, all started by one man with a lawn mower, a fistful of leaflets and an urgent need to pay the rent. Now Jim's was coming to the UK and I could be the first person to get on board. The first person to invest in the world's most successful home services franchise, in the biggest market it had yet entered.

It was all very exciting and I was looking forward to exploring the more entrepreneurial aspects of the opportunity but before I could, I was rostered to spend two days working with Phillip Brooks, a Jim's Mowing franchisee who operated in Melbourne's southern suburbs.

I arrived at Phillip's home the following day, just before eight o'clock and we were soon on the road to our first job. In fact it was our only job, which may well sound like a pretty soft induction, save for the fact we would spend the entire day mowing lawns in and around a huge retirement village.

We drove through and around the village, dropping off cans of fuel and empty grass sacks, as Phillip's three employees were already hard at it. He pulled over and introduced me to the mighty Honda Buffalo, the mower of choice for most Jims. A brief safety induction followed, before he stressed the importance of straight lines, neat edges and let me loose on an unsuspecting nature strip.

There may be no great science to mowing a lawn, but at that moment I was the very embodiment of focus and concentration. I dreaded making a mistake and feared running off the surface into the gutter, bashing the blades and planting what my colleagues call 'donuts' into the lawn. I managed to avert any such disaster, then switched the machine off, emptied the catcher and re-started, setting the throttle to the appropriate speed and blades to a suitable height. I had passed the audition.

For the rest of the morning Phillip worked ahead of me, strimming edges, skirting around trees and garden beds, as I followed with the Honda. He was soon out of sight, as I carried on at a steady pace, catching an occasional glimpse of the others who were all working at a frightening speed.

No one had bothered to tell me we were taking part in some sort of speed mowing championship and I began to feel that I was letting the side down with my careful, inexperienced manoeuvring. I didn't dare rush for fear of making a mistake and besides, I was already exhausted. Lunch time couldn't come soon enough and when the whistle finally blew, I limped to the nearest shop, where I demolished four meat pies and a Mars bar.

I wasn't in any screaming hurry to get back and sat for a few minutes on a seat by the side of the road. Already I could feel my muscles stiffening. I could have taken Phillip aside and said 'Thanks mate, but I reckon I've got the gist of it,' but I don't think that would have gone down too well at the office. Besides who's to say that some other bloke might come out from the UK, and spend a day or two doing the same job?

Well, I wasn't about to be shown up by some Pom.

It was all the motivation I needed. I marched back, fired up the Honda and set out to mow for my country!

I may have been forty but I reckon at that stage of my life, I was about as fit as I have ever been. I had been going to the gym regularly and swimming as often as I could. I was even keeping an eye on my diet. All the same, when I woke up the next morning I could barely move. It was all I could do to lift my head from the pillow. Clearly all that time on a rowing machine in Streatham, with a crazed Albanian gym instructor yelling 'Hudda, Hudda' was scant preparation for hurling dozens of large sacks full of grass clippings into a trailer.

I didn't get up, so much as slid off the bed onto the floor and shuffled into the shower. Coffee, breakfast and more coffee helped, but just how I managed to arrive at Phillip's place on time remains a mystery.

Phillip's staff cracked on at the village while we tended to a few other jobs. Actually he tended to most of the jobs himself, while I listened and observed. Thank God for that.

We even had time to stop for lunch. It was interesting and enjoyable to just sit and chat. Not simply because we weren't working, but because I was able to gather a picture of the Jim's organisation, of the support it provided to franchisees and the camaraderie that existed among them. I came to the conclusion that Jim's Mowing was as much about lifestyle as income and if the work didn't kill me I was certainly going to save on a gym membership.

The second chapter of my induction involved spending a day with Gaynor Andrews, a Jim's Dog Wash franchisee who lived in Eltham.

There are hundreds of Jim's Mowing trailers on the streets of Melbourne, and as distinctive and eye catching as they are, they look like a Leyland P76 alongside their Dog Wash cousins. The Jim's Dog Wash trailer is purpose built in fibreglass. It has its own tank with a rapid water heating element, a hydro bath, blow drier, interior lighting, a non slip work bench and optional sound system. With its smooth lines and bright red exterior, it looks like a scale model of the space shuttle. Well it would if the space shuttle was red anyway.

Our first client was a fat Labrador in Hawthorn. Gaynor collected the client on a lead, led him onto the trailer and into the bath, as I stood watching over the rear 'stable' door. She applied organic shampoos and conditioners, rinsing the client with warm water before lifting him onto the bench where he was given a blow dry, had his nails clipped and was even perfumed. It was simply decadent. He was then returned to his owner (no doubt feeling a new dog), whereupon I imagine he ran outside and rolled in a pile of compost.

Throughout the day we clipped an Old English Sheep

Dog and washed an array of breeds, including of all things a Siamese cat, which looked even more revolting and sinister when wringing wet.

The most interesting episode however, came in response to a job that was allocated by the office. A client in Reservoir was the proud owner of two Pit Bull crosses, both of which needed a wash and worm treatment. I courageously waited next to the trailer, as Gaynor spoke to the client and collected each dog at the door.

'He keeps rubbin' and scratchin' his arse. It's drivin' him nuts' the woman said.

Sure sounded like a candidate for a worm treatment to me.

Gaynor led a powerful, ugly and downright nasty looking dog onto the trailer. It looked like a Pit Bull crossed with a Pit Bull as far as I could see, and I was only too happy to give my friend all the space and time she needed. The wash, dry and treatment passed without incident and Satan was returned to his owner, before Gaynor led Osama onto the trailer. I didn't dare look inside for fear that direct eye contact might instigate some sort of canine homicidal tendencies, but to be fair, both dogs behaved perfectly well throughout. Of course I knew they would.

The following Monday was the first day of Jim's School – Regional Franchisor training at the office.

The first person I saw that day was Greg Puzzolo. He asked me what I had learned during my few days on the road.

'Well I'm not as fit as I thought I was,' I said. He smiled like he knew.

The highlight of the morning was without doubt Jim himself. The face that launched a thousand trailers, spoke quietly and modestly for the best part of an hour. He explained the ethos of the organisation and wrote it large on the white board. 'Find and Keep the Best People.' Rather prophetically, he had (by mistake) used a permanent marker, leaving a clear imprint of the words on the board all week, long after the scent of solvent had dispersed.

We broke for lunch and I was able to chat for while with the man himself. I told him about Sevenoaks and that initially I was just hoping to generate enough work to survive. 'Don't worry about getting the work,' he said. 'There's plenty of work. You need to find really good people as franchisees.' I wish now I had the presence of mind to ask 'And just how do I do that?' After all, he had nigh on three thousand on his books, he should know, but alas, I was distracted by the arrival of the sandwiches.

Over the next few days we covered territory rights, business reviews, advertising and marketing, branding, research and communication. Then we did a role playing exercise. We were split into groups of three and I was teamed up with the roofer and one of the cleaners. Two of us sat back to back, simulating a telephone conversation, while the third sat in adjudication. We were each given a script outlining our own specific circumstances and asked to play different roles. I was cast as a franchisor, calling the roofer on the phone. He was behind in paying his fees and he hadn't been returning calls or attending meetings. In three minutes, I was supposed to address the situation as best I could, whereupon the cleaner would report to the class and give me a score out of ten.

I raised all of the relevant issues in the script but failed to agree a payment plan or secure any commitment to attend future meetings. The cleaner's critique was reasonably kind, before the roofer chimed in, 'Richard's a really nice bloke,' he told the class. 'In fact he's too nice.' Greg wrote the words 'Too Nice' next to my name on the white board.

Oh the shame.

CHAPTER 3

TECHNICAL DIFFICULTIES

I was dressed appropriately for a sunny February afternoon in Melbourne - shorts and a polo shirt and quite absurdly for a cold, wet and miserable morning in London, but I would worry about that in the best part of a day's time.

It was a long flight, rendered more so by the fact the Lauda Air movie schedule was absolute rubbish. I was reduced to watching 'The Fighting Temptations,' if only to appreciate the fact Beyonce can't act, but to my lasting disappointment she was actually quite good.

I entertained myself by collecting as many bread rolls as I could from the flight attendants and hiding them under my tray. I ate most of them between meals, but kept three of similar proportions to juggle outside the toilets.

We stopped in Kuala Lumpur and Vienna before landing at Heathrow, where someone collared me in the baggage claim, asking where I had bought my boots. 'Australia. Bit of a hike from here,' I said, 'cheaper though.'

I shuffled down to the station and caught the tube into town, emerging above ground at Green Park, where it was, as they say 'chucking it down.' Dragging a suitcase and wearing a pair of shorts was no way to tackle weather like this, but I needed to pick up a key to a friend's house where I had arranged to stay. I hanged the expense and hailed a cab.

Once in Battersea I dried off, relaxed and stayed a few days before moving to more permanent temporary digs in Farnborough, where my friend Alexis was living alone in a two bedroom flat. She was moving to Turkey in a month and was grateful for a bit of extra rent.

It was a situation that suited me perfectly. I could come and go as I pleased and although we were some distance from Sevenoaks, I was able to travel there by train and reacquaint myself with the lettings market.

I even secured a one month trial membership at the gym, which I discovered had rowing machines with a programmable pace boat on the monitor. No need for a crazed Albanian here. After some instruction, I was able to set a time and mile rate, which allowed me to effectively race against an oval shaped silhouette. I became engrossed in the 'contest' providing my own radio style commentary, complete with special comments. Sometimes (I fear) out loud.

I caught a couple of trains to London and subsequently to Sevenoaks, secure in the knowledge I would have to come up the equivalent GDP of a small African nation for a security deposit.

The fact that I insisted on a lockable garage limited my options, but I did find a two bedroom flat in a purpose built block on St. John's Hill. Unlike a lot of rental accommodation in the UK it was unfurnished, but by local standards reasonably priced at £800 per month. I dealt with an agent, told some outrageous lies as to my income, forged some employer references and insisted on curtains, whereupon the landlord asked for a twelve month lease, six weeks rent as a deposit, with a month in advance. In the end we settled for £775, and a month's deposit. Which I should think covered the cost of the curtains.

I arranged to move in towards the end of March and spoke with my 'Man with a Van,' a tournament chess playing, Turk called Mr Ugur.

While I was away, I had managed to store all my belongings in a small museum, where I had occasionally worked (oddly enough The Museum of Garden History).

It was situated next to Lambeth Palace, which of course meant retrieving everything at night, once the museum had closed. We parked Mr Ugur's van (illegally) in the forecourt of the Archbishop of Canterbury's residence, thinking it would be downright unchristian to have it towed away, and set about lowering my queen size mattress and base from the roof of the library. It was a difficult enough exercise getting them up there in the first place, but the reverse was something else again. For a time, it seemed to be a question of whether we would crash through the ceiling and subsequently demolish the gift shop or vice versa. Thank goodness for Mr Ugur. His use of straps, ropes, ladders and ramps rendered a minor miracle.

'Mr Richard. We are on the money!'

It was an expression I had used back in December and one he had since adopted as his own. We were 'On the money!' when we had lowered everything down and once again when it was loaded onto the truck. We were also 'On the Money!' as we drove out of London, reached the M25, found the turn off to Sevenoaks and arrived at the flat. I was beginning to wish he didn't speak English.

We lugged everything up the stairs and sat for a moment by the window of an otherwise empty lounge room.

'Mr Richard, you want sofa bed?'

Well, yes I thought, before Mr Ugur told me about a very comfortable, almost brand new sofa bed that I could have for free. All I had to do was help him move some furniture for his friend. I agreed and spent an entire day the following week loading furniture on and off his truck, before I was rewarded with a tattered, stained, mustard coloured monstrosity with one missing leg. No sooner was it sitting in the lounge, than I had arranged to take it to the tip.

Back at Lex's place, I did the rounds of Farnborough's supermarkets and 'Pound Saver' stores, managing to accumulate enough dishes, plates and cutlery, to ensure I wouldn't have to wash up more than once a fortnight. It was far too much to carry on the train and Lex didn't own a car, so I called upon a friend who did.

Ailsa was a colleague from my London temping career who lived in Surrey and drove a RAV4. I rang and explained that I needed her help to move some of my things from Farnborough to Sevenoaks, which from her place in Reigate wasn't too much of a stretch. Not if you are travelling to and from Farnborough in Kent. Of course, I was residing in Farnborough, Hampshire. Confusing isn't it?

We could have picked a better night. It was cold, drizzly and very foggy. It was all we could do to pick out the tail lights of the car in front and the only signs that were effectively illuminated were the ones overhanging the motorway that read 'Fog.' They were about as useful as those that flash 'Congestion' when you are stuck in traffic.

Established in my new abode, I set about creating an office. I arranged to have the phone connected, and before long my 'Welcome to British Telecom Broadband' pack arrived in the post. I followed the instructions to the letter, installing the software for the modem and putting all the plugs in all the right places. The lights were on, but when it came to accessing my email, no one was home. I rang the BT Broadband help desk, which was based in Newcastle. It might as well have been Islamabad, the accents were just as indecipherable. We spent an age reinstalling the modem and altering various settings on my computer, delving into the bowels of the hard drive to places I never even knew existed. Nothing worked. The line was testing okay and we had tried everything short of taking it out to dinner. There was nothing more we could do. BT would have to send a technician out, a process that took some weeks. When he finally did arrive, he tested and monitored the modem, the leads, the phone and all the connections. They were all fine. It wasn't until he went into the lounge that he was able to identify the problem. It seemed that a previous resident had a cable based pay TV subscription, as there was a socket set against the wall with two outlets. I had connected the computer lead to the socket beneath the tiny graphic that looked to me like a computer screen. It was of course supposed to represent a television. The socket a centimetre to its left, the one with the unmistakable telephone graphic, that's where I was supposed to plug the lead in. After several phone calls, hours of adjustment and weeks of waiting, the BT technician was able to fix the problem in less than a second. Of course it's easy when you know how.

Generously, he stayed with me while I connected to the web. Unfortunately, in the process of trying to fix the original problem, I had completely disabled the anti-virus software, firewalls and basically every security setting there was. No sooner did we connect, than my computer was quite literally hijacked. I sat dumbfounded looking at the screen, as some unseen force took total control. Countless pages of unknown origin and dubious content flashed before my eyes. No doubt the virus floodgates were thrown open into the bargain, as before long the entire operating system locked up. I was surprised there wasn't any smoke billowing from the back of the machine.

'Isn't the internet fantastic?' he said.

The next day I caught a train to Tonbridge, carrying my crippled laptop, to the closest computer repairer I could find. I did my best to explain what had happened and basically blamed BT for the whole thing. The bloke behind the counter took charge of the patient and wrote a very detailed, technical memo. 'Reinstall anti-virus, clean up shit on hard drive.'

Even without email access, I was able to make the necessary arrangements to attend the London International Franchise Exhibition and no prizes for guessing who was manning the Jim's stand.

The exhibition ran for two days at the Wembley Convention Centre. Hundreds of franchise businesses had booked masses of floor space and set up their elaborate displays, in order to impress and cajole prospective franchisees.

We hadn't. The Jim's stand was three metres square and consisted of a fold out backdrop with a massive 'Jim's Group' surrounded by logos for each individual division. Apart from that, there was small table, a stool and me, wearing a Jim's Mowing shirt.

It was a difficult two days. No one in the UK had ever heard of us and I didn't feel I knew much more than most of them. Every now and then someone would stop and say 'Tell me about Jim's Group.' I did my best to explain how large and diverse the business was and that I was the first (in fact only) person to come on board in the UK, that I was establishing my own Jim's Mowing Franchise in Kent and hoping to develop the Dog Wash division as well.

'So why should I buy a franchise from you then?' someone asked.

Now I was really stuck. I had rehearsed the general corporate profile piece well enough, but hadn't given a lot of thought to answering what was (let's face it) a pretty obvious question. I think it's fair to say my first few contacts left largely unconvinced, but before long I was in for real shock.

A bloke from Zimbabwe came by, looked me squarely in the eye and all but demanded to know about Jim's. He was assertive to the point of being aggressive and no sooner had I trotted out the bit about my own mowing franchise than he interrupted. 'You'd better put some neat stripes on those lawns boy.'

'Stripes?' I said.

He looked baffled.

'Of course,' he said. 'Plenty of posh people in Sevenoaks, they will all want stripes on their lawn.'

'Whaddya mean stripes?' I repeated.

He threw his head back and laughed aloud. 'You are starting a mowing business in Sevenoaks and you don't know how to put stripes on a lawn?!'

The fact is I had no idea. The answer could have been 'with a brush' for all I knew.

'Oh well,' I said, 'perhaps I'll just concentrate on the Dog Wash business,' which was the most polite way I could think of saying 'bugger off.' It failed.

'Tell me about the Dog Wash then?' he demanded.

Clearly, this bloke wasn't going anywhere. He was having the time of his life watching me clutch at every metaphorical straw I could find. Just for a moment though, I thought I had him, as I waxed lyrical about the trailer - water tank, rapid heating element, blow dryer, non slip bench, stylish exterior, fibreglass. It felt like I was landing a painful blow with each jab.

'What do you do with the waste water then?' he demanded.

Damn. I thought for a moment. 'Well, you just let it out in the street,' I said.

He did that thing with his head again.

'You can't just let out in the street!' he bellowed, 'the Environment Agency will come down on you like a ton of bricks. They'll fine you thousands!'

He walked away.

'Good luck boy' he said laughing.

I doubt he meant it.

The rest of the exhibition was largely uneventful, as I spent most of the time perched on a stool, racking my brain as to how on earth you put stripes on a lawn.

I caught the train to Tonbridge the following week and picked up my laptop. It was working again, but the hijack episode had clearly done irreparable damage. It was now painfully slow to complete even the simplest task and consequently would come dangerously close to doubling as a Frisbee, but for the time being, it would have to do. A new computer was a luxury I could ill afford, given I had to finance a new vehicle, buy all my equipment and keep the nearby Ashique Tandoori in business.

My bank in the UK was called First Direct but it only handled personal accounts, credit cards and mortgages. If I wanted to open a business account I would have to speak with its parent organisation HSBC, which had a branch at the very top of the High Street. I called in and asked to make an appointment with the manager, explaining that I wanted to open a business account and discuss financing a vehicle. I was given a name, an appointed time later that week, and went home to look over my business plan.

I returned a few days later, caught the lift upstairs and met with the relevant individual. I introduced myself, though this wasn't reciprocated, and to this day I can't be sure she was even the person I was supposed to meet, as she didn't bother giving me a business card. All the same, I assumed it was alright to sit down, as she already had.

I slid my business plan across the desk, explaining why I was there and what I hoped to achieve. Jane Doe sat side on, typing my details into a computer.

It wasn't a long meeting. I had only been resident in the UK for a short time and as mine was a start up business, there was really nothing they could do for me.

'We have to do what the computer says,' she said.

I had flown back and forth across the globe, been badgered half to death at the Wembley franchise show and moved into an expensive flat in Sevenoaks. Not to mention prepared a comprehensive business plan and I couldn't even open an account. She looked at me with a blend of disinterest and impatience.

'We used to be able to consider things like that,' she said, 'but these days we just have to do what the computer says.'

I left and soon after composed a detailed letter of complaint that I posted on the 'Customer Feedback Forum' of the HSBC web site. I am still waiting for a reply.

The attitude I encountered at the bank was disheartening, but when I was at the Jim's head office in Melbourne, Greg Puzzolo had told me how helpful and generous Volkswagen (Australia) had been in developing a purpose built Jim's Mowing vehicle. The idea was to house a lockable box on the back of a VW Transporter cab chassis, rather than tow a trailer. I was even there when a bloke from VW handed the keys to Jim, posing for photos and telling him he could pay for that one down the track once he sold it on.

I could hardly wait to meet with their people in the UK. Were they ever going to be excited about Jim's Mowing. Here was a business with 1700 individual franchisees in Australia, entering a market three times the size. We could have a thousand franchisees operating in the UK within five years. That's a thousand new vehicles, and I was the catalyst. These people were going to treat me like royalty. I was looking forward to days out in corporate boxes at Wimbledon, Lord's and Ascot. They might even give me a vehicle for free, just to get the ball rolling. I may have hit a bit of a snag at the bank but Volkswagen, they were going to be all over me like a cheap suit.

I couldn't have been more wrong. In their wisdom, Volkswagen had decided it would supply the vehicles from their commercial dealership located in the geographic centre of the UK. Birmingham.

As anyone from Britain will tell you, people from Birmingham speak with a very distinctive (i.e. horrible) accent. It's very coarse and narrow, the sort of noise you would make if you were to recite the alphabet with an inflated inner tube stuffed up your nose.

I met with two representatives of the VW Van Centre and tried to explain the potential that I believed Jim's Mowing had in the UK. I presented figures that showed the growth of the business throughout Australia, New Zealand and Canada. I projected similar success in the UK and suggested that VW could both supply and finance each vehicle. I explained it was imperative that we get the first one on the road as quickly as possible, the value of branding and the importance of service and follow up.

Their response was to show me a picture of a 'Kombi Van' complete with sixties style 'flower power' regalia, which I imagine was supposed to demonstrate the vehicle's longevity.

I handed them a CD with all the specifications for 'the box,' foolishly accepted their quote as 'inclusive of a substantial discount' and gave them an order right there and then. Little did I know it would be the best part of four months before they would supply.

Chapter 4

A Lack of Local Knowledge

The acquisition of a branded Jim's Mowing vehicle was crucial, not just in operating my own business but in order to recruit franchisees throughout Kent. I had invested in an iconic (albeit Australian) brand and I wasn't about to advertise, let alone present the concept to a potential franchisee without one. Even so I couldn't afford to wait for Volkswagen or the banks to come to the party and decided the only way to get the business going and pay the rent, was to get stuck in.

Phillip Brooks and I had been exchanging emails and he had given me a start up wish list of equipment. With my recently acquired internet access, I set about finding a local supplier and Googled 'Lawn Mower Kent UK,' whereupon I was directed to a retailer on the outskirts of Maidstone.

I walked to the nearby village of Riverhead, hired a van and armed with my West Kent Street Atlas, managed to undertake an estimated forty minute drive across the county in the best part of two hours - the road system in the UK is very unforgiving.

'Palmer's' was more of an agricultural supplier, judging by the fact my mid size van was dwarfed in the company of various John Deere tractors and assorted farm machinery.

I asked to speak with whoever was in charge and was introduced to the Sales Manager. I explained my situation and confessed the fact I had got lost driving from Sevenoaks.

'Sevenoaks?' he said, looking surprised. 'Why didn't you just go to Godfrey's?'

Godfrey's, he told me, was the biggest garden and landscape supplier in the south east and sure to have everything I was likely to need. What's more, it was only a forty minute drive away, given it was located within walking distance of my flat.

Suffice to say I felt a complete fool, but the exercise wasn't a complete waste of time however, as I discovered that one puts stripes on a lawn by using a mower equipped with a roller.

Suitably admonished, I drove back to Riverhead, returned the van and walked home.

The next morning I left my flat and strolled down St. John's Hill, past Blockbuster Video, the Lantern Chinese take away and Sevenoaks Kebabs and Pizza. I crossed at the lights and followed the road as it veered to the right. Within minutes I was walking into the Godfrey's showroom.

Dozens of lawn mowers were spread across the show room floor, while masses of shovels, forks and assorted implements adorned numerous display stands.

Chris Martin was the Manager. He was very helpful, courteous and wore a tie, which I thought was rather extravagant for someone who sold lawn mowers, but he seemed to know what he was talking about, judging by the fact he was across the whole roller mower stripes thing.

I explained what I hoped to achieve with Jim's Mowing and Chris assured me that Godfrey's could supply all of our franchisees with everything that they were ever likely to need, starting with me.

First order of business was a lawn mower. Godfrey's stocked a range of Hondas, but the Buffalo wasn't among them. In fact all the mowers in the UK were configured differently to those in Australia. For one thing, most incorporated a self propulsion system and all (by law) had a blade brake mechanism. My Zimbabwean 'friend' from Wembley had convinced me that the residents of Sevenoaks would insist their lawns were adorned with stripes, so I settled on a Honda mower with a nineteen inch deck and a roller.

What I knew as a 'Whipper Snipper' masquerades in the UK as a 'Strimmer' (apparently Americans call them 'Weed Whackers'). In any case, Chris recommended a Stihl model that featured a 'bump feed' head for the cord, one that could be interchanged with a blade or an adjustable hedge trimming attachment. I was assured that this was indeed the best model on the market, notwithstanding the fact 'Stihl,' is clearly a German word meaning 'Hard to start.'

A blower was added to the list, as were rakes, a spade, a shovel and a fork, before we approached the health safety aspects of the job and added ear defenders and safety goggles. I was happy to follow Chris's advice, as he included spare mower blades, engine oil and a set of spanners, in the unlikely event I would ever actually undertake any equipment maintenance.

I didn't have a bank account, at least not for the business but handed over the Visa card and arranged delivery.

Having made the commitment to buy all the necessary equipment and secure in the knowledge that my friends from Volkswagen would do everything possible to provide me with a vehicle, I formulated my marketing strategy.

I decided to launch my business by means of a leaflet drop and emailed my friend Russell in Melbourne asking him to design me one.

Other than my uniform, Jim's Mowing didn't have any brand presence in the UK, but one has to start somewhere. I asked Russell to place the logo at the top of an A5 size sheet and to feature a list of services and my telephone number. 'We' offered the residents of Sevenoaks a prompt, reliable and personal service for all their garden maintenance needs, and suggested they call 'us' for Lawn Mowing (which I had done for a couple of days in Melbourne), Hedge Trimming (which I had done once for about five minutes), Rubbish Removal (something you don't exactly need a degree for), Gutters Cleared (refer previous), Pruning and Lopping (actually it's probably better you call someone else for that, given there is some chance they may actually know what they are doing) and General Maintenance (whatever that means).

I claimed that most jobs could be done the same day, boasted full insurance cover, offered free no obligation quotes and set about finding a printer.

Google had spectacularly failed to locate one of the biggest lawn mower retailers in the South East, so I decided to deploy a more primitive means of research and flicked through a copy of the Yellow Pages.

Lakeside Printing was located across the street from the station, a fifteen minute walk from my place and the best part of a hundred miles from the nearest lake. Happily they were more adept at printing than geography and before long I was handed one thousand two colour leaflets with Jim's Mowing prominent in dark green.

By this stage all my new toys (I mean equipment), were safely housed in the garage, but short of pushing and carrying them between jobs, I had no means of transport. I rang the VW Van Centre in Birmingham and was greeted by someone with 'that accent.' A feature of the 'Brummie Inflection' is that everyone sounds the same, regardless of age, gender or intellect. It doesn't matter whether they are young or old, male or female, unskilled or professional, they all come across as incredibly thick. Although in hindsight this may have had as much to do with

Volkswagen's recruitment policy.

I spoke with one of the people with whom I had met previously - a fleet sales specialist no less. He told me that as I had been resident in the UK for less than three years, Volkswagen would not provide me with a finance package. They would be only too happy to build and supply, but I would have to buy the vehicle outright or secure finance with one of the banks (not HSBC presumably).

I was staggered and told him as much. From my perspective, I alone would launch the biggest lawn mowing and garden maintenance franchise in the world, into the largest market it had yet entered. For all I could see Jim's Mowing was presenting Volkswagen with the opportunity of a lifetime, the opportunity to supply vehicles to every franchisee in the UK, which given there were already 1700 in Australia, could conceivably number in excess of 1000 within five or ten years. Surely, even for a company as huge and diverse as Volkswagen that was a serious slice of business.

My pitch fell on deaf (to say nothing of dumb) ears.

It was a very frustrating situation but I decided the best way forward was to establish a relationship with a bank that could see the 'bigger picture' and go from there. After all, surely not all of the banks in a country as large and diverse as the UK would be as obstinate and difficult as HSBC.

Perhaps not all, but Barclays, NatWest, Lloyds TSB and Halifax certainly were, as I discovered the 'three year rule' wasn't the exclusive domain of Volkswagen. I contacted my bank in Australia and suggested that I might be able to secure some sort of finance package there but as mine was 'a start up business overseas' – you can guess the rest.

I was embarrassed to find myself in this predicament and having secured the rights to Jim's Mowing and Dog Wash for all of Kent on a strict commercial basis, was reluctant to ask anyone that I had dealt with so far for help.

Eventually I decided to share my frustration with some of the senior people at Jim's Group, only to learn they were collectively involved in a significant 're-think' with regard to the whole UK operation. In fact the Managing Director and Operations Manager both of whom I had met a few weeks before thought so long and hard that they chose to resign, while Brian Duckett and Horwath Franchising - the consultancy firm Jim's had been working with in the UK was unceremoniously sacked amidst a plethora of email sabre rattling and threats of legal action.

It seemed to me as if Jim himself had filed the entire UK venture in the 'too hard basket.' Even so, I had a thousand leaflets and a garage full of equipment, so I set about making some sort of an impression. I donned my Akubra hat, laced up a pair of trainers and hit the streets of Sevenoaks.

I walked up the south side of St. John's Hill and Dartford Road, before tackling both sides of Mount Harry and St. Botolph's Road. There wasn't a single house that had a letterbox on the street. It must be a statutory requirement in the UK that letters are delivered through the front door, which wherever possible should be at the end of a long steep driveway. I was well aware that most of my leaflets would have a shelf life that could be measured in seconds, which made it all the more frustrating to think I was walking up to half a mile at a time to adorn a kitchen bin liner.

As I walked down Woodside (one of several designated private roads), I saw an elderly man tackling the lawn on a steep gradient in front of his house. He was standing about ten feet above street level and propelling a hover mower attached to a rope down what (from his perspective) was surely quite a dangerous slope. He had garnered the distance by wrapping the rope around his wrist and was effectively cutting the grass each time he hauled the machine back up the slope. He was wearing a short sleeved buttoned shirt, tailored shorts, dark socks that measured half his shin and brown leather, lace up shoes. But for a handkerchief tied on his head, he should have been eating a bucket of chips on the Blackpool foreshore.

I walked up the driveway offering him a leaflet. 'No thank you,' he said, clearly focussed on the task at hand. I was convinced he was in the process of killing himself, and all but pleaded to let me help him. I offered to mow his lawns for free, but he was having none of it. 'Go away please. I'm busy!' he shouted, as the mower descended once again.

I leafleted his neighbours and every other house on the left then turned around and repeated the exercise on the other side of the street. Twenty minutes later he was still at it. There was no point giving him a leaflet, I should have offered him a job.

Over the course of the next two days I delivered about six hundred leaflets, each of which featured my home telephone number with a distinctive Sevenoaks prefix, as several people had told me it was important that I be perceived as a local operator. God forbid anyone might think I lived in Swanley.

Mr Creesey was the first to call. He was a retired gentleman with twenty three grandchildren and a house on St. Botolph's Road. I can only assume he concluded that my willingness to undertake 'Odd Jobs' extended to happily risking my life, as a section of his roof had fallen away. I am uncomfortable with heights at the best of times and even though my entire roofing knowledge could be inscribed on the head of a small pin, I made an appointment for 2.00pm that afternoon.

I arrived to find Mr Cressey standing in his front yard. A pair of binoculars hung around his neck. He was staring at the remnants of several broken tiles that had once formed the apex of a roof that sat above three storeys.

I introduced myself and appraised the task in as much time as it takes to turn on a tap. I didn't even own a ladder let alone a crane and wondered if my entire venture could be any more spectacularly unsuccessful than if I was to crash to earth from a height of some thirty metres, while tackling my very first 'mowing' job.

We agreed it was a task that should be undertaken by a

specialist contractor and that given he 'kept himself fit' mowing his own lawn, there was (for the time being at least) nothing I could do for him. He liked my hat though.

I didn't have long to wait for my next opportunity, as I retrieved a telephone message from Jo Breen. Of course, had I remembered to divert incoming calls to my mobile I could saved myself the trouble of walking home before returning to the very same street but no matter.

Jo was the mother of two young boys, she was friendly, attractive and made the best coffee in Sevenoaks. She was English and the coffee Italian.

I continued to mow Jo's lawns every two weeks, until her father retired and proved cheaper than me. I was treated to a mug of coffee each time and often cheered on by her two sons peering through the window and over the back of the couch. I once offered to prune her Privet hedge and was paid without question, in spite of the fact I did a pretty ordinary job and it grew back in less than a month. One day I shattered a window in her conservatory (flicking a pebble with the strimmer) yet she managed to convince the manufacturer it was somehow their fault, rather than let me pay for it.

If all my clients were as lovely as Jo I may still be mowing.

The first time I did a job for her, I arrived in a beaten up old van that I had hired from UK Rentals in Riverhead. The second time I did a job for her (a fortnight later) I arrived in a beaten up, otherwise new van that I had hired from Volkswagen. Inside two weeks I had managed to reverse it into a brick wall, hit a tree and side swipe a concrete bollard in a supermarket car park.

It looked much like any other white van, save for the fact it was adorned with an enormous VW logo on both sides, with the words Birmingham Van Centre writ large underneath. Anyone stuck behind me in traffic could not possibly escape the fact that they could 'Hire this van for £45 a day!' Huge orange and yellow letters made sure of that.

My next lead came from a house in Mount Harry Road. Claire Murray needed someone to trim the conifer hedge that bordered the driveway and to clear out the gutters of her two storey house. I wasn't really equipped, much less insured to work at the heights required, but my detailed risk assessment concluded that the chance of suffering a serious physical injury was far outweighed by the fact Claire had all the attributes of a super model, so I happily agreed to tackle both jobs.

I trimmed the hedge as best I could and was genuinely surprised when she complimented the work I had done. 'It looks fantastic!' she said.

'Does it? You are kidding?!' I replied, stepping in front of the worst of the misshapen sections.

CHAPTER 5

WHAT'S IN A NAME?

Even without a branded vehicle it was abundantly clear to all and sundry when I was working in the vicinity. I dare say the rhythmic scream of the Stihl combi system could be heard in adjoining villages. As if the locals didn't have reason enough to dislike the Germans.

I imagine it was the noise that attracted Claire's neighbour, a woman who effectively owned the other half of the hedge that divided their two driveways. She inspected and (to my surprise) complimented the job I had done trimming the Murray's side and asked if I could tackle hers' and the top. She accepted my quote and I set about the task, finding my confidence with the hedge trimmer growing at much the same rate, as the discomfort and pain in my shoulders. All the same, she was happy with the job and asked if I might undertake a few other things for her.

Quoting jobs is one of the most difficult aspects of

being a 'Jim' and I found myself all at sea when trying to provide an estimate for the various tasks my new client had in mind. I was to clear away a rotten pile of compost from behind a garden shed, remove a satellite dish attached to the side of the house, demolish a stone firewood box, dismantle a number of kitchen cabinets, pull up several metres of carpet and spend an hour or two playing backyard cricket with her two sons. Although to be fair I was happy enough to throw in the last bit.

I had no idea how long it would all take and in the process ignored Jim's First Commandment - 'Thou shalt not provide an hourly rate.' We settled on £25 before I set about dragging several metres of stinking compost into a skip. Over the course of the next week, I came and went between other jobs. I unbolted the satellite dish, dismantled the kitchen cabinets, ripped up the carpet and tried any number of times to deliver a leg break with a tennis ball.

A trip to Godfrey's added a sledgehammer to my equipment collection, which I wielded with some purpose against the concrete firewood box at the side of the house, all the while finding it oddly empowering to systematically demolish something.

I was conscious of the fact I was working 'by the hour' and made sure I didn't waste any time in getting the various jobs done. Needless to say the meter wasn't running for the cricket matches but when I totalled everything up it came to sixteen hours at £25 or £450. I was surprised how much the time had all 'added up' and a little concerned that my client might feel the same way, so as a gesture of good will I amended the total to be £375.

She wasn't unhappy with the invoice, so much as incandescent and quite frighteningly unreasonable. In short, she refused to pay, all but accused me of being a thief and in response to my polite written reminders, commissioned a letter from her solicitor.

I rang her up and suggested that she could pay whatever she thought was a fair amount and that we should leave it at that. A few days later, I received another solicitor's letter. I never recovered a penny, decided to put the whole exercise down to experience and some months later, took great delight in the fact a fallen tree had demolished much of her front fence.

The leaflets that I had been delivering were starting to pay dividends and I was fielding an increasing number of enquiries. One such call came from Mrs Fishwick who lived at 'Mallards' in Linden Chase Road. I made an appointment to look over her property and she gave me a detailed set of directions - 'Eighth house on the right hand side from the corner of Bradbourne Park Road, up the hill and across the street from the entrance to the school.' she said. Number 36 would have done just as well.

'Mallards' was a double storey house built on about a quarter acre block. It had lawns front back, a shed, a greenhouse, a pond, a slope, an array of playground equipment and two massive Willow trees that deposited countless twigs, leaves and sticks on the grass. From a lawn mowing perspective it was like a military assault course.

Undeterred, I quoted £30 to strim the edges, mow the lawns and another £20 to clear away all the weeds that were growing around the pond.

I manoeuvred the strimmer around the swings, trees and trampoline, deciding to mash through the twigs and sticks with the mower. Once I had finished, the lawns looked quite good, whereupon I set about demolishing the sea of weeds that surrounded the pond. There was an abundance of them. Light green in colour and at least a couple of feet high. No matter, I thought, as I waded amongst them in a pair of shorts. The effect was almost immediate. It was a sharp, scratchy almost burning sensation. I tried to ignore it and busily swung the strimmer from side to side, hacking down great swathes of the offensive growth, but before long I was forced into a retreat. I leapt back, dropping the strimmer on the ground, furiously raking my fingers over my legs, oblivious to the fact that my hands and arms were brushing against the very same menace that was already torturing my flesh. I had no idea what was happening. One minute I was strimming a perfectly innocuous bunch of weeds and the next I am trying to literally tear my skin off. It was as painful as it was bizarre.

I tried everything I could to ease the discomfort. Rubbing, scratching, swearing. It only made things worse. I rolled in a garden bed, ran my legs under a tap and smothered myself with grass clippings. None of it made the slightest difference. It was simply agonising but I soldiered on, finished the job and shoved an invoice through the door.

I then rushed to a pharmacy in Riverhead and worried that they wouldn't take my symptoms seriously, described everything in great detail. I need not have bothered. Apparently I had discovered Stinging Nettles, a relatively common feature of the local landscape and the horticultural equivalent of the Box Jellyfish.

I would have happily paid that pharmacist a thousand pounds to alleviate the agony. As it happens, I parted with less than a fiver, which is probably just as well, as the creams and lotions that I liberally applied, made not the slightest impression. I went home, hopped in and out of the bath (which only made things worse) and paced back and forth, completing countless laps of my flat, throughout what was an entirely sleepless night.

Happily the physical symptoms began to subside the next day and I ventured out to quote a mowing job in Vine Avenue.

Mr Vaudrey was an older gentleman and a nice man. His house (as were most in the street) was absolutely huge and built on a large block of land. Suffice to say, he needed someone to mow the lawn. I thought the job was worth £40 but quoted him £30. Even so, he seemed quite shocked. 'Goodness me' he said. 'That's rather a lot. Mr Clark used to do it for twelve.'

'Twelve pounds?!' I said in disbelief, surveying a back garden the size of Old Trafford. 'You're kidding?' I said.

'No. Twelve pounds,' he assured me.

It was a job that (even with a ride on) could not

possibly be completed in less than an hour, which given the fact I would have to collect and dispose of all the clippings as well, made £12 an absurdity. It begged the question however – 'Just where is this Mr Clark and why isn't he doing it now?'

'He can't do it. He's in hospital,' Mr Vaudrey said. 'He's got pneumonia.'

I said that I wasn't the least bit surprised and soon after we settled on £30.

I completed the job and we chatted over a cup of tea before he referred me to a neighbour who owned an even bigger property and was in a similar bind. It came as no surprise that Mrs Forbes – Hamilton (not her real name) was also a client of Mr Clark. On this occasion we were out of sync forty five pounds to sixteen, a prospect that she could not countenance.

'I can't possibly pay that,' she protested, to which I replied that 'I can't possibly do the job for any less.'

'Well, what on earth am I supposed to do then?' she demanded.

I suggested she move into a flat. It was a remark she either didn't hear or simply chose to ignore as to my astonishment she told me to go ahead.

Two hours later I finished the job, gratefully accepted her cheque and thereafter designated Vine Avenue a 'No Go Area.'

My next call was in response to Mrs Martin who lived in Woodside Road. Her property was called 'Ashbury,' which could be found on the left hand side after turning right from Mount Harry Road, just beyond the second speed hump. I followed her directions to the letter and discovered that 'Ashbury' was also the house with a large number 8 attached to it.

Meeting Mrs Martin was like being introduced to the mother of one of your mates from school. She was pleasant and friendly with a confident, authorative manner. Her previous gardener had 'moved on' and she was anxious for me to spend an hour and half there every fortnight, mowing the lawn and doing various bits and pieces. There wasn't much grass to mow and the rear of the property was on a steep slope but I was encouraged by the fact that if we scheduled the job for Thursday mornings, she would rarely be home and could leave instructions with her cleaner. I thought £25 a time was too cheap but agreed all the same. I mean you don't argue with your mate's mum.

Dealing with Mrs Martin worked out quite well. Her cleaner was indeed always there and armed with a set of written instructions. I spent some of the time mowing but most of it weeding garden beds, raking up leaves and cleaning out gutters. More importantly however, I could always count on a cup of tea.

Before long I managed to attract the attention of the neighbours. Mrs Cole lived opposite 'Ashbury' and Sally Ann Boult next door. Both became regular mowing clients which meant I could now complete three jobs without having to move the vehicle. Mrs Martin's £25 wasn't such a bad deal after all.

Mrs Cole's property was flat and relatively easy to

mow, although after I had butchered the edges of her lawn with the strimmer, she insisted I use her own set of shears instead - a minor blow to my professional pride. Sally Ann's property was by contrast, every bit as steep as 'Mount Ashbury.' The back garden was two tiered, which meant lugging the mower up a long set of timber steps to a kind of Everest Base Camp, before making a final assault on the summit.

By this stage, I was starting to build a healthy client base and making some new friends along the way. The weather had been quite good, but I was still driving around in a hired van, I didn't have a business bank account and above all no idea as to what was happening with the whole Jim's foray into the UK.

CHAPTER 6

THE CARRICK DRIVE
CHAINSAW MASSACRE

I had by now all but given up on financing a vehicle through Volkswagen and every bank that I had approached wasn't the least bit interested in dealing with me.

I thought perhaps if I spoke to an accountant I might (at the very least) be able to solicit some advice and was recommended to a local firm called Greenaway.

I rang their office and was introduced to one of the partners. I explained my situation and before long had an appointment for later that week.

Bob Lovitt and I met over a cup of coffee in an Italian bistro in the High Street - across the street from his office and certainly a less formal surrounding.

I explained how I came to be presented with the Jim's Mowing opportunity, how huge and diverse the business was in Australia, to say nothing of my own lofty ambitions for the south east corner of the UK.

Bob listened, took notes and gave me the impression he was genuinely interested. Which of itself was something of a revelation.

I shared my frustration of dealing with the banks and how important it was that I finance a vehicle. He said I shouldn't worry and that he would speak to a contact of his at HSBC. I vowed not to hold my breath and we shook hands.

The following week I had my second appointment with HSBC. This time I managed to reach the top floor where I met with Bob's contact. Jeremy Thompson had spent his entire working life with the bank and was a matter of weeks away from a well earned retirement. Clearly ours wasn't going to be a long term relationship but the mere fact I was sipping tea in the manager's office was a pretty good start.

The age old adage as to who, rather than what you know certainly rang true that day. I don't know what Bob told him but the bloke couldn't do enough for me.

I probably spent less time in that office than I did when meeting with any other bank. The difference was that this time I left, not with a burning sense of frustration, but with a new business account and a vehicle finance agreement.

Thanks to Bob, things were looking up. I walked down the High Street, rang the Brummies at Volkswagen, told them to get a move on and retrieved a couple of messages from my mobile that promised some more work.

The first message was from Lisa Pullen, who had retrieved one of my leaflets from her letterbox at Carrick Drive. Lisa was a slim, attractive mother of two young children. True to the Sevenoaks stereotype, she drove a massive four wheel drive. As you do, when you have to negotiate a couple of speed humps on the way to the shops.

Lisa gave me the impression of someone with too much time on her hands. She employed a full time nanny and seemed to have no shortage of ideas as to what to do next with the house and garden. For one thing, she seemed to have a local builder on some sort of retainer and as she and I strolled around the garden together, it was clear she had some ambitious plans. As to whether or not I (with all of six weeks' experience) was the best person to be carrying them out was another matter.

The first task I undertook was to help her builder to dismantle, reassemble and relocate a timber garden shed. It was a structure I think we moved all of about four feet.

Next up, I was to clear away a mass of tangled shrubs and small trees growing in a corner of the property, so as to make way for the installation of an elaborate timber climbing frame for the children.

Some of the branches and trunks were quite thick and beyond the capacity of my existing tool ensemble, which could mean only one thing - chainsaw.

It was an exciting prospect and one I fairly leapt at. I had never used a chainsaw before and oblivious to the fact that I was as likely to sever a limb as a branch, I went shopping.

I arrived at Lisa's house the following morning and soon after made a detour to Godfrey's, where I had purchased a brand new Stihl model the previous day. I stood on the shop floor, resplendent in my Jim's Mowing uniform, thinking that I had never seen the showroom so crowded. It was fairly brimming with customers, residents of Sevenoaks and its surrounding villages, all potential clients and advocates of Jim's Mowing. At least that was until Manager Chris Martin spotted me and called out 'What? Can't you start it?!'

As embarrassing as it was for a garden and landscaping 'professional,' there was no disguising the fact. My brow fairly dripped with perspiration, my cheeks were flush and hair dishevelled. I was holding the chainsaw in my left hand, as my right arm had entered some kind of spasm, having tugged countless times at the rip cord in a vain attempt to start the motor.

'No' I replied sheepishly.

Chris kept me waiting while he served a customer. A process I have no doubt he extended for comic effect, as he could barely contain himself when he approached and ushered me outside.

We stood in the car park and I handed him the chainsaw, insisting it was faulty.

Chris put it on the ground, braced it with his foot and adjusted the choke. He tugged three times on the cord, concluded that the motor was flooded and then all of a sudden, amidst great palls of smoke and the stifling odour of petrol, he had the audacity to start the damn thing.

He revved the throttle a few times (as if to labour the point), sending the chain spinning around the bar at a rate of knots - all the while alerting the fact to everyone within a five mile radius that single handed, he had saved the day. Show off.

Chris explained the role of the choke (as if I was six years old) and gave me a crash course in the nuances of the Stihl MS 230, before I drove back to Carrick Drive with a renewed sense of purpose.

I carried the chainsaw into the garden, placed it on the ground and braced it with my foot, just as Chris had done. I switched the choke a third of the way on, tugged twice on the cord and then took the choke off. I prayed silently and tugged again. The MS 230 roared into life. Revving it triumphantly, I adjusted my safety goggles and ear defenders, before crawling beneath the prickly branches of a sturdy Holly tree, ripping through its trunk like a hot knife through butter. I found it quite thrilling, as I set about its secondary trunk, the one sprouting from the turf a few inches to the right. To this day, I wish I had taken note of the fact that the bark on the trunk (of what I thought was effectively the same tree), was clearly different to the original. It was smooth by comparison and lighter in colour, but it wasn't until I dragged it from the tangled mess that I realised my mistake. As I pulled the base of the trunk towards me, I looked across and aghast, as a celebration of lilac disappeared into a sea of dark green.

My new chainsaw had been in operation for less than two minutes and even though I myself was still physically intact, in the blink of an eye, I had managed to ruthlessly execute Lisa Pullen's fifteen year old Rhododendron.

I thought it desperately unfair that the base of a plant was anchored at least six feet from where its foliage actually protruded. I think that's what those in the legal profession term 'contributory negligence.' All the same, it was the one element in the entire project that Lisa had specifically asked me to protect, or at the very least retain.

I hauled the evidence across the lawn, dropped it on the ground and started piling the other cuttings on top of it, in a desperate and futile attempt to conceal my crime. I thought perhaps if I took the visual element out of the equation, Lisa might be so enthralled by the exciting expanse I had created, that she might forget that she ever had a perfectly healthy, plant growing there in the first place. Like that was going to work.

I had the presence of mind to switch the chainsaw off, as I saw her walking towards me. In the event she decided to attack me with it, I figured I could probably cover about three blocks before she got it started.

I really should have owned up and taken full responsibility, but to my everlasting shame, I chose to 'play dumb.' My flimsy, awful defence was that I didn't realise she hadn't wanted the tree murdered in the first place. In any case, I suggested that my 'scorched earth policy,' would afford her two children even more room to play. That they would (as a consequence), grow up to be even stronger, healthier and more rounded human beings than they otherwise might - a kind of 'big picture' scenario.

I was amazed and relieved when she reacted in an almost Zen like manner. She didn't scream and she didn't cry. In fact she didn't even raise her voice. She appeared quite calm and philosophical. Moments before I was convinced that my Jim's Mowing career was over. Now it was as if the Governor had telephoned conveying a full pardon, just as the executioner was about to throw the switch. I could have kissed her, but instead simply cleared away all of the rubbish, cleaned up the site and moved on to my next adventure.

Mr Raisen lived at the top end of Wildernesse Mount. He had seen my advertisement in the Sevenoaks Chronicle and thought perhaps I 'could have a look at doing a few jobs around the garden.' He sounded like an ideal client. Friendly, getting on a bit and (a fact confirmed by my West Kent Street Atlas) quite close by.

We arranged to meet and I arrived at his house (a quaint rural cottage) at the appointed time. There was a car in the driveway but no answer when I rang the bell or knocked on the door. I was wary of proceeding any further, lest I discover that Mr Raisen bred a particularly aggressive strain of Doberman, but given the small timber gate a few feet to my right was hanging off its hinges and restrained by a piece of twine, I concluded that was unlikely to be the case.

I opened the gate, placed it back on its hinge, fixed the

twine and strolled around the side of the house, walking past a conservatory that looked out over the garden. I stood in the open doorway, where I could clearly see two people inside. Mr and Mrs Raisen no doubt, both smartly dressed and fast asleep.

Not wanting to induce a heart attack, let alone two. I coughed, cleared my throat and walked back to the front door, trying to make relatively polite, but discernible noises as I went. I knocked on the door again. There was no answer.

I walked back to the conservatory to see them both still slouched in their respective arm chairs. I wondered if perhaps they had died simultaneously – a harmless, elderly couple, done in by the shock of a particularly spiteful headline in the Daily Mail.

Happily that proved not to be the case, as after I had spent fifteen minutes beating the living daylights out of his front door, Mr Raisen finally opened it.

'Ah. Jim's Mowing!' he said excitedly.

'Yes. Mr Raisen. How do you do?' I replied.

He shook my hand and looked at his watch. It was a quarter past three.

'Sorry I'm late.' I said.

He stepped outside, ushered me through the gate and towards the conservatory, where he introduced me to his wife, (now wide awake) who also reminded me of the fact that I was 'late.' I apologised and made a mental note to invest in an air horn.

Mr Raisen, whose checked sports jacket, tie and

trousers contrasted with my scruffy shorts and boots, took me on a tour of the garden. He escorted me down onto a lawn that resembled the 15th at Augusta. An expansive, undulating fairway complemented by a water hazard. He called it a pond. It looked more like a lake to me.

In any case, he and his wife had long enjoyed the fact that migrating wild ducks would nest there for a couple of months in the autumn. The ducks hadn't turned up for a couple of years, apparently due to the plethora of weeds that now clogged the water. A close inspection revealed that a mass of thick dark coloured weeds were indeed thriving. So much so, there was barely a patch that wasn't affected. I can only imagine what it looked like from the air.

The weeds themselves were suspended beneath the surface. They weren't actually anchored to anything, let alone rooted to the bottom and as such it was relatively easy to drag them out with a rake. Mind you, there were a lot of them.

My mission was to wade in and clear out as many as I could. Given the weather had been quite warm, it was a job that appealed as a kind of final act refresher. I could mow lawns, trim hedges, weed and rake throughout the day, then spend an hour or so waist deep in cool water. I offered to come twice a week in the evenings for as long as it took, Mr Raisen agreed and we struck a deal.

I had spent much of the time that we were walking in the garden doing some mental arithmetic, calculating a quote to mow the lawn. It was a big enough job for me and surely beyond a man of my client's advanced years, but to my surprise, it was the one task he was determined to complete himself. Instead he gave me a long list of things to do. It included digging over the rose garden, clearing out the borders and painting all the drain pipes at the front of the house.

I offered to tackle the rose garden then and there. Firstly because it didn't look to be a particularly big job and secondly because when Mr Raisen's asked me to 'clear out the borders' he had made it quite clear that I should leave all of the Heather intact. Given I had no idea which plants were in fact 'the Heather,' I put that task to one side, until such time as I could find some sort of visual reference on the internet.

The rose garden itself was arranged in a circle, set inside some paving stones just outside the conservatory. I fetched a fork and spade from the van and set about making short work of all the weeds and a few dead stems.

With Mrs Raisen an interested spectator, I thrust the fork into the soil with some gusto, whereupon it rebounded with enough force to jar my shoulder and almost break my wrist. I dropped the tool, grabbed hold of my arm and recalling the fact my elderly client was within ten feet, exclaimed 'Goodness. That's a bit firm!' Needless to say 'firm' wasn't the first four letter word that sprang to mind.

It was a salutary lesson. I had given the Raisens a fixed and modest quote to dig the garden over, thinking it would take less than an hour. What I hadn't realised was the fact the soil was so dry and compacted it was like concrete and probably why all of the roses had long since died in the first place.

I had no option other than to continue, though it was a painfully slow job, not helped by Mrs Raisen's constant supervision (from the comfort of the conservatory), as I scraped, clawed and bashed for the next three hours. Eventually, I managed to clear every weed and each dead rose, whereupon I called it a day, went home and fell asleep in front of the TV.

The next morning I met a new client who lived across the street and down the hill from Jo Breen in St. Botolph's Road. Her house was located at the top of a steep, narrow driveway and her garden was a bit of a mess. The lawn was long and patchy, low branches hung over the drive and the borders resembled a tropical jungle.

There was enough work there to keep me busy for months, but Mrs Birt only wanted me to come once a fortnight for a few hours at a time. I had hoped to stick to the principal of giving a fixed quote for each specific job, but given that strategy had failed so spectacularly the previous day, I agreed to an hourly rate and offered to start immediately.

My first task was to clear the garden beds of weeds and other undesirables.

Mrs Birt pointed to a number of plants and reeled off a few Latin names of the species she 'obviously' wanted to protect. None of them were all that 'obvious' to me, so I suggested that if she could tell me which ones were the weeds, I would happily pull them out. She laughed for a moment, before realising that I was in fact serious, whereupon she gathered a fistful of clothes pegs and Post It notes, attaching them to the plants that I should leave well alone.

It was an embarrassing admission, but I wasn't about to masquerade as an expert. Not after the 'Carrick Drive Chainsaw Massacre' anyway.

She left me to carry on and I worked fast and hard. Before long, I had a huge pile of waste in the back of the van and had made a discernible difference to one side of the driveway at least. I was quite proud of the job I had done and above all she was happy. So much so that she asked me to tackle the lawn at the back of the house and clear away some weeds from around the pond.

The back lawn was quite flat but punctuated with obstacles like swings and pet enclosures.

I set about strimming the edges and parts of the lawn that the mower couldn't reach, quite oblivious to the fact that I must have absolutely terrorised the two Guinea Pigs taking refuge in their hutch.

I made a good a fist of the grass and was looking forward to actually completing a job without any discernable drama, when I set about weeding the rocky border to Mrs Birt's pond. It was only small and there weren't even that many weeds, but access was tricky, as some of the rocks were loose and slippery. I had pulled out all but one when I made the mistake of reaching across the water to complete the final act. It wouldn't have taken any great effort to simply walk around the other side, but to my cost I chose to lean over, placing the toe of my boot on a timber trellis that stretched across the pond itself, sitting just above the water level. A sliver of pine gave way and my foot plunged in, whereupon I over balanced and fell forward, executing a spectacular belly flop. I crashed into the pond, destroying the trellis (probably squashing a couple of goldfish) and got a fearful soaking in the process.

I was unhurt but clearly had some explaining to do. I gathered the broken pieces of timber, tossed them and all of my equipment in the back of the van and knocked on the door.

Given the fact I was thoroughly drenched, I could have probably spared Mrs Birt much of the detail as to exactly what had happened, but I gave her a full account of the incident, together with an apology.

As it happened, she was well aware of just how rotten and fragile the trellis was. She had placed it there years before when her children were much smaller. A safety measure, in the event one of them was foolish enough to fall in presumably. In any case, she had wanted to get rid of it for some time and I had in fact done her a favour.

'No worries' I said, 'any time.'

CHAPTER 7

DON'T MENTION THE WAR

I was steadily building a good base of clients, but from both a practical and marketing perspective it was imperative that I had my proper sign written Jim's Mowing vehicle on the road. I rang Volkswagen in Birmingham to check on its progress and was assured everything was 'under control' and that I could expect it in a couple of weeks. I was particularly anxious, as I had been contacted by a potential franchisee in Kent and I didn't particularly fancy turning up for a meeting in a hire van.

In the meantime, a new client had been in touch and I had an appointment to meet with her that morning.

Nicola Gill lived in The Oast House at Nearly Corner in West Kingsdown - one of the district's more interesting addresses.

She had two jobs in mind for me. The first of which was mowing the lawn. In the past she had an arrangement with a local fellow, who did a few people's lawns for some extra cash, but he had recently bought a new car and his wife wouldn't let him put the mower in the back. The second job was a bit more involved and it required a site inspection of 'the shed.'

Nicola's shed was located in the far back corner of the property. As far as I could see the overall structure was solid and sound, but the roof was absolutely shot to bits. It was full of holes, rotted through in places and in the process of collapsing. A process I managed to accelerate (to my cost) by poking a particularly damp section with a broom handle, while standing directly underneath. Mind you, the roof itself (what was left of it anyway) was nothing more than sheets of particle board, covered with a supposedly waterproof felt.

Nicola wanted to have the roof replaced. She and her husband had put their house on the market and a neat, practical and intact garden shed was only going to add value. By the same token, she didn't particularly want to spend a lot of money getting it fixed, so I proposed demolishing what was left of the roof and replacing it with sheets of particle board, covered with a supposedly waterproof felt.

I didn't dare climb on the roof, as I didn't particularly fancy the prospect of being a human wrecking ball and did my best to measure the task from ground level. I made a few notes, drew a diagram and took everything to the Wickes store in Otford.

Before long, the old roof was no more and I was soon piling damp, rotten piles of mush in the back of the van, replacing them with brand new sheets of particle board.

It wasn't until I was fitting the third and fourth sheets that I struck a bit of a snag. I had carefully measured the overall dimensions of the roof, but what I hadn't taken into account was the distance between each of the joists that I was laying the sheets across. The first row overlapped by a few inches, which was all well and good, but the second would be lying over just the one, and only a couple of inches from its edge at that. Ultimately it might look alright to the eye but woe betide anyone who had occasion to walk on the roof, as I for one wouldn't be taking the short odds it would hold. I thought of pulling up the first row of sheets and sawing them off so that they could effectively share the same joist but trashed that idea when I realised I would be wasting a lot of material and subsequently buying more.

With the first two sheets nailed down, I lifted up each subsequent one, laying them over the joists, trying various combinations and arrangements in search of the most secure and cost effective option. Like a giant Tetris puzzle.

It was quite an exercise to manoeuvre such large sheets into different positions and having squashed a couple of fingers in the process, I came to the conclusion that it was (after all) only a shed.

I reverted to my original design and once I had all the sheets in place found that only two of seven rows were perhaps not as secure as I would like. Even so, I still had to get up on the roof to nail them all down, a process I undertook with the utmost care.

Attaching the felt would present more of a challenge. I had bought three large two metre wide rolls and each was very heavy. I climbed up a ladder, lifted the first roll onto the roof and set myself to roll it all the way across in one fell swoop - a distance just shy of eight metres.

Perched on a middle rung, with my waist level with the roof, I rocked back and forth a couple of times (as a means of building momentum) and heaved as hard as I could.

It rolled about a foot.

I reached over, drew it back and tried again, with a similar outcome.

The felt was so thick and so heavy it would only roll a few inches at a time, whereupon I resorted to using a 'beached whale' technique in order to roll it out. I lay face down on the roof, trying to spread my weight across as large an area as possible, nudging and pushing each roll a little bit at a time. I dare say I looked quite silly, not that anyone could see me, but the fact is I was too scared to care in any case. I was constantly worried that my next shove might be my last and that at any moment I would come crashing down through the roof and into the shed, to be impaled on a rusty garden tool.

By now it was getting quite late, but I was determined to finish the job, lest the wind slip under the felt overnight, deposit it all on the ground and undo much of my hard work. I crawled and wriggled across the roof, tapping a hammer as I went, trying to sound out the joists. I emptied an entire packet of roofing tacks and secure in the knowledge that the felt wasn't going anywhere, I climbed down stood back and admired my work.

I thought it looked like a first class job and told myself so. Mind you it was quite dark at the time.

The next day, I had an appointment in Shoreham, a small and rather quaint village a few minutes from Sevenoaks.

Shoreham sat either side of a stream and boasted a pub that was built in the sixteenth century - a time (judging by the height of the ceiling in the bar), when the average man stood little more than five feet tall.

My client was Mrs Franklin – White, an elderly widow who had been married for many years to a famous artist – someone I was clearly expected to have heard of.

She was a painter herself and although (by her own admission) not as good as her late husband, she continued to conduct workshops and training courses under his name.

She lived in a large two storey house, set amidst what was once a fabulous and picturesque garden. No doubt it had proven both an inspiration and a bountiful subject in the past, but sadly it had long since overgrown and was now littered with nettles, brambles and all manner of horticultural nasties.

Though quite frail, Mrs Franklin – White was a cantankerous character who complained time and again that other gardeners she had employed would turn up once and never return. The latest culprits were 'two young men from the golf club' who promised they would come every fortnight. I felt sure that she had simply scared them off, but even so, it wouldn't come as a great shock if one day their remains were discovered in her hidden cellar, drugged and hacked to death with their own tools.

Presenting a quote to Mrs Franklin – White was always an adventure. I would arrive and wait by the door while she located her walking stick. She would then escort me to a particular section of the garden, where she would explain exactly what she wanted me to do.

I would then present her with a quote.

She in turn would reel back in horror, insist that I must have made a mistake and go on to complain about how much things had gone up since the war. We would then move on to another part of the garden, repeat the exercise and so on.

Unlike my predecessors, I did return and over time managed to clear all of the paths so that she could at least stroll around what had become of the garden.

I was even extended an invitation to an exhibition featuring some of her work and that of many of her students. She was genuinely surprised and seemed quite thrilled when I showed up, taking me by the hand and conducting a private tour.

Most of the works were for sale and I was handed a price list, whereupon I too was shocked as to just how much things had gone up since the war.

CHAPTER 8

A CUP OF TEA AND A TETANUS SHOT

I started the day by ringing the Volkswagen Van Centre in Birmingham, and after suffering through a detailed account of my contact's long weekend at the seaside, I was asked (not for the first time) to confirm that the dimensions of the purpose built box and the angle of the mower ramp on the vehicle were in fact okay. Given I had handed the same bloke a set of detailed specifications and drawings (several weeks before), it was clear to me that his question was merely a tactic to justify the fact that delivery would be further delayed. I even managed to crack the VW code, translating his assurances, such as 'We want to take the time to make sure it's exactly what you want' to 'we really are pretty useless and haven't got a clue what on earth we are doing.'

There was little more I could do, so I hung up the phone, loaded the hire van and set off to see a new client who had responded to my ad in the Chronicle.

Mrs Stigger was in her nineties and lived with her daughter in Bull Finch Lane, Riverhead. She was a very friendly, gentle woman with whom I probably spent as much time drinking tea and eating biscuits, as I did mowing her lawn. She was a Lieutenant (an Intelligence Officer), during the Second World War, who farewelled her Spitfire pilot fiancé one morning, never to see him again. It was an episode that occurred almost seventy years ago but one that was clearly painful for her to recall.

Befitting someone with her gentle nature, Mrs Stigger had a habit of adopting and housing 'rescue dogs.' Animals that had often been neglected and ill treated in the past. She would have two or three living with her at any one time, which (given dogs do what dogs do) presented its own set of challenges when it came to looking after the lawn. Let's just say I soon learned to keep my mouth shut when using the strimmer.

I arrived to mow the lawns one day, well aware that Mrs Stigger had recently made the difficult decision to have one of her ageing and arthritic Border Collies put down. What I didn't realise, is that she had managed to replace it (almost immediately), with a tortured psychotic. Without doubt the ugliest and most evil dog I have ever seen - a powerful, thick set mongrel with a dull, matted coat and bright yellow eyes.

We first met when I quite innocently opened a gate leading to the back garden. A split second later its jaws were wrapped around my leg, its teeth buried in my flesh. I have no idea how it may have been treated in the past and at this point I didn't much care. I was just grateful for the fact that it responded and recoiled after being punched in the head.

The dog let go, just long enough for me to leap back, cry out in pain and pull the gate shut. Mrs Stigger had heard the commotion from the kitchen. She had come outside and ushered the dog in. We then carried on a rather perverse conversation. Each of us either side of the gate, where she did her best to assure me that everything was fine and where I did my best to explain to her that I was in fact bleeding quite freely. Eventually, I was granted leave to visit the Sevenoaks Hospital and assured that a cup of tea would be waiting for me upon my return.

A tetanus shot, some antiseptic and a couple of gauze patches later, I was back in business and attending to my regular clients as if nothing had happened, although I did put off my evening dip in Lake Raisen for a week.

By this stage I was starting to get some referrals from existing clients to their friends and relatives, which was certainly encouraging and one such instance introduced me to a man who lived in Wrotham.

Mr Taylor owned a small property that backed onto a forest. His front and back lawns were immaculate and the gardens well kept. At first glance, I didn't see much of an opportunity, given that he was clearly capable of making a good fist of things himself. That combined with the fact that he seemed to regard me with a degree of suspicion.

We stood in his back garden, he with his arms folded, as he asked me no end of questions about Jim's Mowing. I trotted out the well rehearsed corporate history, but stumbled when it came to my own qualifications and experience. He was curious to know the attributes I was looking for in a franchisee. I didn't think for a moment that he was interested, but thought perhaps he might know someone who was, so I explained that practical skills and experience counted for little. 'Communication and the ability to deal with people are paramount' I said. 'Anyone can learn how to mow a lawn, but you can't teach someone to be honest, reliable and hard working.'

He seemed surprised to learn that I wasn't necessarily aiming to recruit qualified gardeners and that there really wasn't much of a horticultural aspect involved in our initial training.

Even so, he said he was looking for someone to commit to a weekly schedule of maintenance, alternating lawn mowing with weeding and general tidying of the garden beds.

I explained that I was more comfortable giving him a quote for a specific job, than I was providing any sort of hourly or half day rate, but managed to dodge the issue by assuring him that I would check my diary and send him a written quote in the post.

He accepted the arrangement and then presented me with the details of a specific job that I could perhaps give him a quote for.

The branches of a number of trees were growing over the fence that bordered the rear of his property and he needed someone capable and qualified in the use of a chainsaw to cut them back and consequently provide him with a supply of firewood for the winter.

I thought it sounded like an ideal opportunity. There was no confusion as to which tree or branch to cut and all I had to do was follow the line the line of the fence, lop off the branches, cut and stack. Easy.

'No doubt you've got your CS30 and 31,' he said.

I confessed that I had no idea what he was talking about.

'Your certificates of competency,' he said. 'You aren't allowed to operate a chainsaw in the UK without them.'

'Well I have,' I said.

He made it quite clear that under no circumstances should I be using a chainsaw, that my insurance policy would not cover it and that no retailer even had the right to sell me one.

I suggested that he was mistaken, as I had in fact purchased a chainsaw recently, although to be fair to the people at Godfrey's, I seem to recall telling them that I had used one several times before. This was of course completely untrue.

He stood his ground, adamant he was in the right, whereupon I asked just how it was that he knew 'so much about chainsaw qualifications anyway?'

At this point, I had of course ignored the long standing legal tenet, never to ask a question that you don't already know the answer to, whereupon it transpired that Mr Taylor had recently retired from his position as Chairman of the Independent Agricultural Contractor's Association.

I sent him a letter the next day, outlining a schedule of work and costs to maintain his lawns and garden. He wrote back, thanked me for my time but politely declined. I can't imagine why.

That evening I had an appointment to meet Tom Harker - my very first franchise prospect.

I showered, changed and arrived at The George and Dragon in Lamberhurst, wearing a Jim's Mowing polo shirt. I met Tom in the bar and we sat down over a couple of pints.

He had 'come from work,' dressed in jeans and a shirt splattered with paint and plaster.

After being made redundant from a stock broking firm in Tunbridge Wells, he had been renovating a couple of houses, while considering a franchise investment. Whatever he might decide to do in the future, it was clear that after an eight year stint 'in the market,' a return to the corporate world didn't particularly appeal.

I explained how it was that I had come across the opportunity and that being from Melbourne, I couldn't help but be aware of the phenomenal success that Jim's had achieved.

Conscious that I had no real experience of the Jim's franchise system, to say nothing of the fact I had arrived in a van emblazoned with VW Van Centre Birmingham, I stressed the fact that it was 'early days for us in the UK' and tried to focus the conversation on what I knew of the operation in Australia.

It was clear that Tom had been doing his research. I

was impressed with how much he knew of Jim's, if a little deflated to learn that he was on the verge of signing a franchise agreement with a company called Lawn Master.

The UK franchise market was awash with lawn treatment opportunities. I had seen plenty of other lawn mowing and garden maintenance franchises in Australia, yet none that offered a specific lawn treatment service. Oddly enough, the reverse was true in this part of the world.

As far as I could see, the Lawn Master regime amounted to spreading fertilizer on clients' lawns throughout the course of a year. It wasn't particularly physical or varied, but perhaps that was the appeal. I couldn't knock it, as any lawn treatment franchise that I could name (and there were several) was already bigger, longer established and dare I say, more successful than me.

Tom explained Lawn Master's territory structure (which was nowhere near as good as Jim's) and outlined his ambition to have a multi vehicle operation within five years.

It was a difficult pitch to counter, given he appeared committed, focussed and seemed to have a more clearly defined business plan than I did. I really didn't have a shot to fire, so we had another beer, talked about something else and agreed to keep in touch.

Later that night I sat down in front of the computer and after checking the latest AFL news, downloaded an email from Jason Jaap.

Jason was an experienced Jim's Mowing franchisee and

a regional franchisor in Melbourne. He had been involved with the company almost from its inception and had recently been appointed by Jim to effectively re-launch the business in the UK.

It was the first bit of news that I had received in weeks and a clear indication that perhaps the UK operation hadn't been forgotten after all.

Jason had already booked himself a flight, as he intended making a fact finding trip to the UK in a few weeks time. It was an exciting prospect and with the knowledge and experience he would undoubtedly bring, exactly what the business needed. I replied to his email, said I was delighted he was coming over, offered to collect him from Heathrow and extended an invitation to stay in my flat.

CHAPTER 9

SQUIRRELS

It took four months, several meetings, numerous phone calls and no end of exposure to Birmingham accents, but my custom designed vehicle had finally arrived.

I was relieved to see that it did in fact adhere to the specifications I had supplied. Everything that was supposed to open and shut did. There was a ramp that folded down for the mower, shelved units along the side and a large enough area at the back to throw all of the waste. The cab itself was white and the box on the back painted 'Brunswick Green,' with Jim's bearded face and all the associated livery in a bright and distinctive yellow.

There was just one last thing to check.

The drawings I had been given in Australia, allowed for a padlock to be fitted to the mower ramp, but they didn't specify any locks on the shelving units. As a consequence, I had made sure that I rented a flat with a lockable garage, so that I could leave all of my equipment safely in the vehicle overnight. I had confirmed its dimensions several times and measured them against the width of the garage door beneath my flat. According to my calculations everything should fit, but there was only one way to be sure.

The first journey I undertook in my new Jim's Mowing vehicle, was one of about thirty metres, where (after a couple of three point turns), I managed to line up the open door of my garage and drive more or less straight in. With the top of the box fitting safely under the door and the nose of the cab resting just short of the wall, I checked in both side mirrors to confirm that the tail was safely inside. Mission accomplished.

Not quite.

Working from a written set of specifications, I had checked the width of the vehicle against the garage interior, but failed to take account of the fact that I would of course be seated behind the wheel at the time. An oversight that became clearly apparent when I first opened the door, as it travelled all of about four inches before hitting the wall. It was a similar scenario on the passenger side and as I sat in my brand new, purpose built vehicle, it soon dawned on me that (given I hadn't exercised a sun roof option), I was effectively trapped.

I felt a complete fool, but rather than bid an immediate and embarrassing retreat, I spent the next few minutes tuning the radio (just in case someone was watching) and the next couple of years loading equipment in and out of the garage at the start and end of each day.

Having eventually come to terms with the ramifications of my miscalculation, I called upon a new client who had seen one of my leaflets.

Stephanie Beattie lived in a terrace house on St. John's Hill - a stone's throw from my flat. She worked as a freelance journalist, did occasional voice over work and was studying for a degree in astrology.

Her house was adorned with a massive, tangled Wisteria that crowned a front garden that consisted of two hugely overgrown shrubs, set amidst a number of concrete slabs, loosely covered in tiny coloured pebbles.

It may have been a small garden but the list of 'things to do' was long, as Stephanie asked me to dig out the two shrubs, sweep up all the pebbles, lift up the slabs, lay some new turf, plant a couple of small hedges, prune the Wisteria and fit some chicken wire to her wrought iron railing fence.

None of the tasks particularly fazed me with the exception of tackling the Wisteria. It certainly needed attention, as it was already wrapped around various telephone cables and disappearing beneath the gutters and roofs of two adjoining houses. It looked as if it was trying to wrestle the buildings to the ground, but my client was more concerned with the fact the plant had failed to produce any flowers for the past few years. Mind you, she was somehow under the impression that she had 'an expert' on the case, so apparently that was the least of her worries.

I started by sweeping up the pebbles and shovelling

them into thick plastic 'rubble sacks' before lifting each slab, disturbing a hidden, subterranean world populated by crawling insects and bugs.

I cut down the two shrubs, dug out the roots and turned over the soil with a fork when a passing neighbour stopped to speak to me. He asked if I was taking on any more work and if so, could I knock on his door two doors up? I assured him that I would, just as soon as I had finished, whereupon he enquired 'how much do you charge anyway?'

'Heaps,' I replied.

He seemed a bit surprised and suggested that if that was the case, then perhaps he should find someone else.

'I would,' I said.

I think he realised I was kidding.

Thereafter, my first real foray in my Jim's Mowing vehicle was to Richard Abel Landscape Supplies in Sundridge, where I had ordered a few metres of turf to lay in Stephanie's front garden. The turf itself was grown in Norfolk and cost me £2.00 a metre. Had I bought it in the nearby Select Garden Centre (whom Richard also supplied), the exact same stock would have cost me £4.95 a metre. Quite a mark up, but it had of course travelled across the road by then.

Richard Abel was a specialist wholesale supplier who made me feel quite privileged, given I was 'in the trade' and consequently able to solicit much cheaper prices and plenty of advice.

I even managed to bump into a couple of Australians

in the car park, who seemed almost as excited at the sight of the vehicle as I was. They had no idea that Jim had spread his wings this far and asked me how big the operation was in the UK?

'Well, it's pretty much just me at the moment' I said, but true to form they thought that was 'great' and wished me every success.

I returned to Stephanie's house, laid the turf and watered it in. I thought it looked terrific and I was thrilled at the transformation. Happily so was she and chock full of confidence, I vowed that tomorrow I would tackle the Wisteria.

As luck would have it, one of my neighbours had given me a book entitled 'Pruning,' some weeks before. It had a couple of pages solely devoted to Wisteria, with a detailed instruction of how and when to prune, and an illustration of a plant that looked nothing like the one I was confronted with. The one in the book had a neat uniform shape, with a handful of lateral vines shooting from a central trunk. By comparison, Stephanie's Wisteria looked as if it should be on some sort of medication.

I studied the text meticulously and the next day tackled the job with an extension ladder, a pair of secateurs and a sense of foreboding. I might have done just as well with a whip and a chair. 'Pruning' outlined a method that should ensure great bunches of flowers burst forth the following spring, but it was difficult if not impossible to follow when my first priority was simply to tame the beast. Thick sinewy strands invaded every tiny crevice, clinging fiercely to cables and siblings alike. For the first hour or two, I threw the text book out the window and simply hacked the vine into a vaguely manageable state, before trying to deploy some of its more subtle principles.

When I had finished, Stephanie's Wisteria bore little resemblance to its former incarnation. It was practically bald and neatly confined behind a series of wires that I had since stretched across the front of the house. Its thicker branches punctuated by short 'off shoots,' all pruned back to the third bud.

Only time would tell whether or not the operation had been a success and I must have studied that Wisteria's progress dozens of times over the ensuing months, aided by the fact I had to pass Stephanie's house on my way to the Chinese take away. By early spring I could see a few buds forming and I watched intently as they swelled and grew. Before long the entire vine was draped in a mass of plump grey pouches. They seemed to be hanging from every stem, until one day they all burst forth in a spectacular festival of colour.

At that stage, my business card featured a list of services printed at the base. Garden Maintenance, Hedge Trimming, Rubbish Removal and the like. I was seriously thinking of adding 'Wisterias a specialty.'

Buoyed by my recent success, I made an appointment with Mrs Phillips who lived in Hitchen Hatch Lane. She had picked up one of my leaflets and rung me at home the night before.

Mrs Phillips had lived her entire life in the company of

her mother, much of it in their current abode - a house (appropriately enough) named 'Squirrels.'

Young Mrs Phillips (as I referred to her) was sixty five, while her mother, Nasty Mrs Phillips (as she once referred to herself) was ninety three. They became an intellectual sideline for me, as I spent no small amount of time (over the next couple of years), trying to decide which of the two was the more insane.

When I first pitched up at 'Squirrels,' it was Young Mrs Phillips who answered the door. She was short and plump with grey hair, cut and shaped into a 'bob' that sat above her shoulders. She wore thick spectacles that magnified her eyes to a frightening degree and spoke with a high pitched shrill, fuelled by generous amounts of saliva.

'Yes!' she shouted, staring at the embroidered logo on my shirt. 'Jim's Mowing! Yes! Hello!'

'Who is it Susan!' came a quivering shout from the lounge room.

Holding the door open, Young Mrs Phillips looked over her shoulder and screamed 'Gardener Mummy!'

'What?!' came the reply.

'Gardener Mummy!' she shouted back.

The exchange continued for some time before Nasty Mrs Phillips (protesting that she couldn't hear) waddled out of the lounge. Propped on a walking stick she stood next to her daughter.

Young Mrs Phillips shouted in her mother's ear 'Gardener Mummy!'

Nasty Mrs Phillips fixed me with an angry stare and pointed with her stick.

I hadn't even introduced myself before she let rip with a tirade of abuse. She had been let down in the past by gardeners who hadn't shown up, or who had quoted a job, only to present her with an invoice for an amount in excess of what had been agreed, or added VAT, trampled the flower beds, kicked the dog, scratched the car and pretty much ruined her life.

I expressed my sympathy for the appalling treatment she had been subjected to in the past and assured her that I would do everything in my power to complete any job I undertook to her complete satisfaction.

She didn't believe a word of it and quite frankly neither did I, but at least we managed to move on and debate the cost of mowing the lawn.

Presenting a quote to Mrs Phillips x 2 was like trying to negotiate a mass redundancy with a couple of militant trade unionists. I suggested thirty pounds - a quote that was greeted with absolute derision. Given there was a tall Pine tree growing in the middle of the back lawn, depositing no shortage of cones on the grass (all of which would have to gathered up before the grass was cut) the job was probably worth forty, but I had to factor in the entertainment value of dealing with two of the district's more colourful characters and we finally settled on twenty five.

I had managed to establish something of a rapport by this stage and agreed to do the job there and then, when

Nasty Mrs Phillips put me firmly in my place. She stepped forward onto the porch and with the handle of her walking stick resting in the crook of her wrist, put her right hand on my arm. She raised her left and pointed at me with her index finger, wagging it inches from my face, as she chided me 'Now. You listen to me young man. You are a colourful Aussie, but a very naughty boy!'

I took what I needed from the vehicle - strimmer, mower, safety goggles and especially ear defenders, whereupon Young Mrs Phillips was kind enough to give me a crash course in lawn mowing. She even showed me how I could adjust my own equipment. Apparently, if I lowered the height of the deck on the mower, I could cut the grass a little bit shorter. Gosh, thanks Mrs P.

I set about strimming the edges as precisely as I could and carefully raked up every single Pine cone before mowing the lawn with the neatest and straightest lines I could manage. I was about two thirds of the way through, just coming up the slope, when I could see Nasty Mrs Phillips wobbling across the terrace.

I mowed up to the top of the lawn, pretended that I couldn't see her, turned around and came back down. I stopped at the bottom of the garden and emptied the contents of the catcher into a sack, hoping that that she might get bored, go back inside and fall asleep. No such luck.

I slowly pushed the mower towards her, pausing at every opportunity, hoping that she might turn her back, just long enough for me to execute a swift U turn and run back down to the bottom.

There was nothing I could do, she had me cornered and I simply couldn't ignore her any longer. I walked to the top of the slope and tried to act surprised when our eyes met.

'Hi Mrs Phillips' I said smiling.

Nasty propped herself on her walking stick, her right hand shaking furiously, as she gestured towards the front of the house.

'Can't you make a better fist of that front lawn?!' she shouted, furiously. 'It looks absolutely dreadful!'

She was clearly unhappy, but I was gravely offended. I mean I may not be the most experienced, qualified or even capable gardener, but I wasn't about to stand there and have the quality of my work questioned in such an ill informed and aggressive manner.

I reached forward and switched the throttle off on the mower. I stepped towards her, looked her squarely in the eye and said 'I haven't done it yet!'

'Oh,' she said.

CHAPTER 10

AN OFFER I COULDN'T REFUSE

Conceptually, the M25 motorway makes perfect sense. It's a four lane ring road that encircles Greater London and feeds the various tributaries that snake their way to all points of the country. The problem is that everyone else knows that too and as a consequence, it can quickly transform itself into the world's biggest car park. The day that Jason was due to arrive in the UK it was the road to Heathrow. Many times (both before and since) it has been the road to hell.

I joined the party at Junction 6 and was relieved to see that the traffic was moving freely but heavy enough to generate some useful exposure for the brand. Short of its delivery from Birmingham, this was effectively the Jim's Mowing vehicle's public launch. Painted bright green and gold, it was impossible to miss and I waved politely as the other cars sped past, thinking that perhaps my first franchisee might be seated behind the wheel.

Jason's flight was on time and after a cup of coffee and a couple of laps of the terminal, I saw him emerge from immigration and customs. He was dark, stocky and understandably tired.

It was by now mid afternoon and I was anxious to hit the M25 before the peak hour mayhem, so we made use of the mower box for Jason's suitcase and hit the road.

Together, we shared something of our history with Jim's on the way back to Sevenoaks. Jason's measured more than a decade, while mine had (to date) lasted a matter of months.

After leaving school, he had worked as a clerk for a customs agent and having long harboured an ambition to work for himself, seized the opportunity to become one of Jim's very first mowing franchisees. He made a great success of the business and later invested in a regional franchise that covered much of North West Melbourne. After selling that on, he had helped to start the Jim's Trees division and had worked his way up through the ranks again, although he did point out 'that was five years and about fifteen kilos ago.'

Jason and Jim were quite close and occasional squash partners, which I found really encouraging. Together they had seen the business become a huge and diverse network, that spanned the entire country and I couldn't see any reason why we shouldn't be able to achieve something similar in the UK.

Once we arrived at my flat, I put the kettle on and introduced Jason to the sofa bed, before ducking out to finish a couple of regular mows.

One of those regular jobs was for a young Swedish couple who lived at the top end of Hitchen Hatch Lane - out of range for Young Mrs Phillips and just around the corner from the ill fated Lisa Pullen.

Matthias had been seconded from Stockholm to work in London, while his wife Ida stayed at home looking after baby Elvira and the biggest dog I have ever seen.

Ida stood outside the front door cradling her sleeping child in her arms, all the while assuring me that their Great Dane was 'still only a puppy,' as he stood on his hind legs, his paws resting on my shoulders. Being quite tall myself, I have often found it slightly unnerving to meet someone who is as lofty as me. Never before had I met a dog that was, let alone one that had the capacity to eat my head.

I wondered if the dog was perhaps a manifestation of Scandinavian pride, as Ida proudly proclaimed that Elvira was named after the title character in the 'famous' film.

Not wanting to broadcast my ignorance of Swedish cinema, I quickly fetched the mower from the vehicle and set about mowing the lawn. The grass was quite long and damp in patches, where the branches of a couple of fruit trees hung over it. Some of the apples that they dropped were huge and though often rotten, they made good footballs, as I conducted a series of penalty shoot outs into the garden beds.

I had to be careful strumming and mowing the Swenson's lawn, as I often found myself concentrating too much on neat edges and straight lines, rather than the branch of the tree I was about to collide with - episodes that were as infuriating, as they were painful. All too often I found myself rubbing my head and cursing. Needless to say, any apples that fell as a consequence, I didn't so much place in the top corner of the net, as launch against the fence.

Returning to my flat, I was pleased to see that Jason was still awake and had made himself at home. I left him busily typing an email, while I rustled up a bog standard Bolognese. Hopefully his body clock would allow him a decent night's sleep, as the next day we would be attending to some of my regular customers.

We started at Jo Breen's house in St. Botolph's Road, before doing the Woodside Road circuit that consisted of Mrs Martin, Stella Cole and Sally Ann Bolt. For the most part Jason strimmed while I mowed, which provided me with an interesting insight as to how well and how quickly two people could work together from one vehicle. That combined with the fact Jason wielded the strimmer like a wand. When I strimmed a client's edges, I was grateful not to kill anything, or at the very least not to scalp the lawn, whereas Jason raced around with the sort of precision that suggested that he had been doing it most of his working life – which (to be fair) he had.

There may have been an embarrassing gap in our respective skill sets, but it was still a worthwhile exercise, as there were some simple tips Jason conveyed, that would help me to work a little more efficiently and that I could hopefully (one day) pass on to a franchisee.

We spent the rest of that week working together and much of the next, which gave Jason a modest insight into the UK market and me a better understanding of the Jim's system and structure.

We would mow lawns, do quotes and shift the odd piano during the day and talk all things Jim's at night. Before long though, it was time to do battle with the M25 and make a return trip to Heathrow.

A few days after he got back to Australia, Jason sent me an email. He was still very much committed to developing the business in the UK and suggested that perhaps we would be better off working together, rather than he operate on a 'national' basis with me solely responsible for Kent. He proposed that I relinquish the rights to Kent and instead take a 30% stake in the UK business. Thereafter, we would try to sell a minority share to a group of investors whom (it was hoped), would provide a sufficient amount of working capital for us to effectively launch Jim's Mowing throughout the UK. He attached a copy of a prospectus that spelt it all out and it seemed to stack up pretty well to me.

I emailed him back and said 'Thanks for the offer. Let's go for it.'

CHAPTER 11

CRASH AND BASH

My new vehicle was already paying dividends. It was eye catching, distinctive and a very effective marketing tool. People were stopping to speak to me in the street and it was certainly a lot more practical when it came to loading equipment on and off, to say nothing of the fact I could cart all the rubbish in the back. Above all though, I felt proud to be behind the wheel and all the more confident when it came to quoting jobs and dealing with the occasional awkward client.

The only downside was that as Jim's Mowing was a 'commercial enterprise,' I wouldn't be able to use the local tip any longer. At least not the domestic section anyway. I had been travelling there every week (at least), for a couple of months, always managing to convince those in charge, that the rubbish I was disposing of was indeed mine and from my own property. Clearly the fact that I was unfailingly dressed in a Jim's Mowing uniform wasn't enough to undermine that.

From now on though, I would be classed as 'trade' and required to dispose of my green waste in a hitherto hidden and uncharted world - a dark and sinister chasm, concealed behind the domestic façade of the Sundridge Household Waste Disposal Site.

Entering the trade section was like stepping onto the set of a science fiction film. It covered about three acres, with massive piles of processed waste stacked thirty feet high. Mountains of muck that had been crushed, mashed and fast tracked as fertilizer. I drove slowly past each one, as a thin vapour of deodoriser wafted from a series of jets mounted on the perimeter fence.

The entire area was patrolled by a single 'tip monster.' Dark, unshaven, surly and ugly, he operated a front end loader, scooping up great swathes of waste, shifting them about and arranging them into different piles. He didn't speak, so much as grunt and every day, seemed determined to be even more rude and arrogant than the last. I think he probably lived there, making his home in one of the many compost mountains, existing on a diet of month old fruit and rotting vegetables. It came as no surprise one day to learn that he was a Millwall fan.

In the far corner of the plot there was a single pile of raw green waste. I backed the van up, opened the rear doors and lowered the tail gate, so that I could add the contents of my own cargo to the pile. I had done a couple of garden clean ups during the week and the vehicle was full of spiky brambles and branches, all tangled and tightly packed, having been repeatedly stomped upon by a middle aged Australian in a pair of size thirteen Blundstones.

To my surprise, the 'tip monster' offered to help. He had seen me struggling to extract so much as a twig from the back of the truck and rather than me spend the rest of the day engaged in a kind of garden waste 'tug of war,' he suggested that we run with his idea. It was a simple enough plan. He would 'drop' the fork of his loader into the back of my vehicle. Once it was firmly wedged in place, I would drive a few feet forward, whereupon all (or at least most) of the rubbish would end up on the ground.

Well it seemed like a good idea at the time.

At first, the monster didn't manage to get much of a purchase on the waste, so I reversed and we tried again. This time we had a measure of success. I could feel a great weight lifting from the back as I drove forward. I stopped, got out and was delighted to see that that we had managed to deposit about half the contents of the bin on the ground.

If only we had stopped there.

Unfortunately, we decided to try one more time. I sat in the cab with the engine idling, while the monster manoeuvred the loader into position. I am not sure exactly what means he used to control the movement of the fork, but can only assume he didn't call upon his brain to any great degree.

All of a sudden there was an almighty crash and I was hurled around the cab, banging my head on the ceiling. I flung open the door and jumped out, just as the monster was reversing from the scene of the crime. He blamed the wind and the fact that I had driven off too soon – an ambitious claim given the vehicle was in neutral with the hand brake on. In any case, he had managed to plunge the fork into the back of my (now no longer new) vehicle. There were deep gouges in one of the rear doors, both sides of the bin were dented and splayed, to say nothing of the fact it was now impossible to close the tail gate.

It was an ugly sight. Only a work vehicle to be fair and little more than a steel frame with painted aluminium panels, but I still wanted to cry.

I dragged the rest of the rubbish out by hand and surveyed the damage. The box was still more or less intact, though badly scratched and misshapen.

The 'tip monster' climbed down from his machine, shrugged his shoulders and produced an acrylic strap, complete with hooks, buckles and some kind of a bracket. He fixed a hook over the railing at the top of the box, stretched the strap across the other side and started to winch the two together. At first, I didn't expect him to achieve anything, but was pleased to see the box slowly return (after a fashion) to something like its original shape. Before long, I was able to shut the rear doors and close the tail gate (albeit with the use of my shoulder).

It was a strange feeling, thanking someone for carrying out a rudimentary repair to a vehicle he had so recently obliterated, but given there wasn't another tip for miles and I had no other viable disposal options, I couldn't afford to start an argument. Anyway, we all know what those Millwall fans are like.

I drove away from the tip trying to put the whole episode behind me, fearing all the while that it would in fact be the box that ended up behind me, as owing to the recent trauma, it might break free from the chassis and crash onto the road.

Happily that didn't happen and I managed to arrive with the vehicle intact, at Mr and Mrs Young's house in Dartford Road. Given they lived within walking distance of my flat, they had received one of my leaflets through their front door and I had been mowing their lawns for the past couple of months.

Dartford Road was an extension of the Sevenoaks High Street and rather than leave the vehicle outside, I chose to drive in and park on the Young's pebbled driveway.

I managed to open and shut all of the side doors and mower ramp okay, extract the necessary equipment and complete the task, before starting the engine and heading off to the next job.

Rear visibility wasn't great in the vehicle (as I only had two side mirrors to work with) and I was definitely still angry about the recent incident at the tip. At least those were the two excuses I adopted, shortly after reversing into the Young's verandah.

I managed to break the corner of a tile that sat between a brick and timber post. More aesthetic than structural but given it was just outside the front door, impossible to miss. Given the last time I was there I had managed to demolish a terracotta plant pot (being a bit careless with the leaf blower), I could really start to sense my reputation (such as it was) being undermined.

Neither of the Youngs were at home, so I raced to Wickes and bought a small bag of cement (not bothering to solicit any advice) and set about trying to repair the damage. I would of course confess to the crime in any case but was anxious to do what I could to lessen its impact.

Having absolutely no knowledge or experience of bricklaying, to the extent that I didn't even realise that I should have been mixing the cement with other materials such as sand, the exercise was a complete waste of time.

I left a note (the gist of which was 'I'm afraid I've done it again') and decided at that point, to call it a day. I drove home, put the cement in the garage (where it stayed for the next few years) and sat around feeling rather sorry for myself. That evening, I bought an expensive bottle of wine, presented it to the Youngs (together with an apology) and an offer to mow their lawns a couple of times for free. They were both very reasonable about the whole thing and accepted quite graciously, whereupon I walked home. After all, I dared not drive.

The next day, the most extraordinary thing happened. Lisa Pullen rang.

I felt sure she must have dialled a wrong number. I mean until I had arrived on the scene, she had been the proud owner of a perfectly healthy, colourful and thriving Rhododendron, yet bizarrely enough she did indeed actually want to speak with me.

Lisa had decided to re-design and re-plant much of her

garden. Even though she had employed a professional horticulturist to select an array of suitable plants, she wanted me to do much of the preparatory work. I was both surprised and delighted to be given the opportunity and we made an appointment to discuss the project.

I arrived at Lisa's house the next day and we strolled around the back garden, managing to avoid any mention of the 'chainsaw incident.' Her plan was to build up the existing garden beds with extra top soil and re-plant them, before dressing the lot with chunky pine bark chips.

My job was to extend some of the beds, re-turf a few small sections of lawn, cart in and rake over the soil and bark. Something even I should be able to manage.

As we wandered past one section of the garden, Lisa explained how she intended to prune and shape a couple of shrubs and a small tree that was encroaching on her children's cubby house.

It was a simple enough job and one she had left out of my original brief.

'I can do that for you' I said enthusiastically.

Lisa leapt between me and the plants in question.

'No you won't!' she said, extending her arms, as she shielded me from her precious garden. 'I know what you're like!'

I thought it was fair enough.

Before long, I was back at Richard Abel's, ordering two tonnes of top soil and three cubic metres of bark chips. Logistically, the job was going to prove a bit of a challenge, as gaining access to the garden in order to deliver the soil wasn't so easy. Lisa's property backed onto a quiet street and Richard and I concluded that it might just be possible to lift the bags of soil and bark over the fence and lower them into the garden using the crane fitted to one of his flat bed lorries. As long as we could pull up close to the kerb, it shouldn't be a problem and given the garden beds would be empty, all we would need to worry about was clearing the fence.

Timing would be an issue however. Sevenoaks is very much a commuter town, with many of its residents and those of the surrounding villages, making their way to its station each weekday morning, on route to London. Strict parking restrictions applied close to the station but Lisa's house was on the fringe of the free parking zone. Consequently, if the London commuters got there ahead of us we wouldn't be able to pull up next to the kerb. As a result the crane wouldn't be able to reach over the fence, which would leave us no option other than to leave the bags of soil and bark on the footpath. I would then have to wheelbarrow everything through the back gate and up a set of steps, which needless to say was far from ideal.

Richard and I hatched a plan.

He would load the lorry first thing in the morning and be 'on site' by 6.30am. I would meet him there acting as a guide, while he operated the crane. The idea was to pull up next to the kerb before the commuter cars arrived, but just to make sure. Richard loaned me a number of traffic cones that I could set up in the street the night before. That way I could cordon off an area large enough for the lorry to pull in, just in case some of the cars arrived before we did.

It seemed as though we had all the bases covered. I drove up the night before and placed each of the cones in position. I set my alarm for 6.00am and was on site as Richard's lorry pulled up. His driver did a good job getting into the street at all, as it was already clogged with parked cars, including the stretch that I had so carefully cordoned off. Some of the drivers had clearly chosen to ignore my request but one or two had been kind enough to collect each of the cones and stack them up next to a tree, so not a complete loss.

We were left with no other option than to lower each of the bags onto the footpath, as the arm of the crane couldn't possibly reach over the fence from the middle of the road. Richard's driver operated the crane as I stood by.

'Mind the fence!' I said any number of times, 'but scratch as many cars as you like!'

Our plan had failed but at least we had affected delivery of all the materials. The issue now was how best to transport everything to the other side of the fence. Rather than shovel the soil into any number of wheelbarrow loads and then negotiate a path through the back gate, I decided to simply launch it over the fence a spade full at a time. The garden beds were clear, so I wasn't likely to destroy any plants and as long as I didn't throw the soil across the lawn or bury a small child, I should be okay.

Once the soil was safely on the other side of the fence, I could rake it across the beds, before launching three cubic metres of bark chips in a similar fashion.

I adopted a back hand stance, digging into the soil and hurling the contents across my right shoulder. A couple of early excursions into the garden confirmed that the soil was landing safely and well within the confines of the garden bed, so I ploughed on. The novelty of throwing soil over a seven foot fence wore off pretty quickly and it was really quite depressing to see another huge bag of soil sitting right next to the one I had barely made an impression in already. I decided that I would rake the soil out after every twenty or so throws, just to break the monotony and eventually emptied the first sack to a sufficient degree that I could drag it inside and tip what remained onto the garden.

I now had one cubic metre of soil either side of the fence and I raked what I had thrown smoothly and evenly before setting about the second sack.

It was hard work but eventually I managed to get all of the soil and all of the bark on the other side of the fence. The beds were nicely built up and I was really pleased how it all looked, as I watered the bark down with a hose. That was when I first felt the pain in my wrist. I imagine the various muscles and tendons in my arms were cooling down by this stage, aided perhaps by the odd splash of water but I was surprised that I hadn't detected any discomfort before now. The pain in my right wrist was such that I couldn't even hold the hose, let alone turn off the tap. What's more it was only getting worse. I cradled my arm in the tail of my shirt, gathered all my tools and the empty sacks, before making my way to the minor injuries unit at the Sevenoaks Hospital (again).

I was of course already registered (courtesy of Mrs Stigger's psychopathic canine) and was grateful that someone was able to attend to me more or less straight away.

I hopped up on a bench, explained what I had been doing and how quickly the pain had arisen, whereupon a nurse massaged and probed my hand and wrist. She didn't think any bones were broken but as she prodded and probed the joint itself we soon arrived at an impasse.

'Tell me if this hurts?' she said.

Her query was greeted with a resounding 'Yes!' as I violently squirmed and writhed across the bench.

She diagnosed 'Tendonitis,' gave me an information leaflet and explained (with the aid of a wall chart) that hurling two cubic metres of soil over a seven foot fence was not something the human wrist was actually designed to do.

Rest and a course of anti- inflammatory tablets should follow. I was okay with the second bit but couldn't see much future in the first, whereupon I was fitted with a brace that bound an aluminium strip to my arm, by means of three Velcro straps.

I joked that perhaps I should take up Ten Pin Bowling, not realising at the time, that brace and I would be spending several months together.

CHAPTER 12

THE BEST FORM OF DEFENCE

One of the great testaments to the marketing power of my vehicle was how many neighbours of my existing customers became clients themselves.

Such was the case in Bradbourne Park Road where I had done a couple of mowing jobs for a woman who lived in a Housing Association property, when her elderly neighbour approached me just as I was loading my equipment.

'Know anyone who does Mowing?' she asked.

I was standing about two feet to the left of a massive Jim's logo and replied 'Well, oddly enough me.'

We walked back to her property and she explained how she lived in the downstairs section of a semi detached corner house. A portion of the front garden was her responsibility to maintain, as was most of the back. Her name was Mrs Marsh - Annie to her friends and Mad Annie to me.

From the outset, it was clear that she was quite a character. For someone so old and frail, she had tremendous energy, a wicked sense of humour and a thoroughly stubborn demeanour.

She asked me for a quote to mow her front and back lawns as 'West Kent Housing had been on her back about it.' She was clearly living alone and probably on a pension and given I already had a client next door, I quoted her twenty pounds for a job that was (to my mind) worth thirty.

'Oh no' she said emphatically, shaking her head from side to side.

I thought her reaction was pretty harsh but before I could justify the price with my usual preamble of strimming edges, collecting and disposing of clippings, full insurance cover and so on, she blurted back 'Forty.'

'You're not supposed to haggle up,' I said, but she insisted, explaining that she wanted to make sure I would do a good job and that I would keep coming back. I assured her that each time I did, I would find a few other jobs to do (of which there were many), so I could be sure she was getting value for money.

She agreed and put the kettle on, as I went to fetch the mower.

I became a regular fixture at Mad Annie's and over time maintained her entire garden. She wasn't exactly shy when it came to airing the 'family laundry' and there were certainly times when I could have done with a little less detail regarding her recent operations and visiting Welsh boyfriend. All the same forty pounds in cash was always placed under a porcelain figurine in her lounge room, which I generally retrieved after a cup of tea and a sandwich.

We spent a lot of time talking and I was often reminded that she wasn't exactly fond of her neighbours. She tore strips off 'the one on benefits' next door, 'the bloody cow upstairs' and 'that evil witch' across the lane. By the same token, she was extraordinarily generous to me and it was rare that I ever left her house without clutching a soft drink or a bottle of wine.

I soon learned how important 'scheduling' was when it came to working for Mad Annie. She lived a few hundred metres from the entrance to the Bradbourne Park Primary School and to find a parking spot within a reasonable distance of her house during the afternoon school run was a physical impossibility. Being Sevenoaks, every week day at 3.00pm the road would be clogged with a fleet of late model four wheel drives. It was as if an invasion force had gathered outside the school gates, to receive its final orders before the assault on Orpington.

The one day I was caught out and I had no choice than to park several hundred metres away. I pushed the mower along the street and carried all of the tools that I was likely to need. I managed to finish the job (and my tea) before the heavens opened, but oncc they did it was (as the locals say) 'absolutely chucking it down.' I didn't particularly fancy getting a thorough soaking, so I gathered all of my equipment together, left it on the corner of the street outside Mad Annie's house and made a dash for the van.

I drove back and parked on the corner of a narrow lane that bordered her property – admittedly on a double yellow line. I had lowered the ramp, lifted the mower inside and opened the side shelving units, when I first met Annie's neighbour - the one who lived 'across the lane.'

She was wearing a heavy black raincoat and holding an umbrella.

Suffice to say, she was less than impressed that I had parked where I had. I tried to explain that my vehicle was originally parked about half a mile away and that I was simply trying to avoid getting a drenching, but she was having none of it.

She became hysterical and marched towards me screaming something about 'ignoring civic responsibilities.' By this stage, I was already soaked to the skin and responded that if I didn't have to spend so much time trying to explain myself to her, I probably would have finished and left by now.

All of which didn't make the slightest impression, as she stood (safely dry), shouting at me from little more than a foot, while pointing at the two yellow lines painted on the ground.

She fixed me with a furious stare and spat 'What if an ambulance had to get through there?!'

I loaded my last piece of equipment on the van, slammed the door shut, turned towards her and said 'Well madam, if it was coming for you. I don't think anyone would care.'

Oddly enough, the same school that was inadvertently the cause of that altercation in the first place became a client itself, or at least a part of it did. The local council was supposed to maintain the grounds surrounding the Acorns Nursery School but they had proven so unreliable and their service so poor, that I was contracted to the task.

It was a tricky job, as I had to negotiate a path in and around an array of climbing frames and playground equipment, while my performance was carefully monitored by an audience that some weeks reached double figures.

I could never see or tell what activities the teachers had assigned the male children in particular but whatever it was, it clearly paled in comparison with the spectacle of a man with a lawn mower.

The first time I tackled the job with a class in session, I glanced over my shoulder to see someone looking at me from the window. It was a little boy with his hands raised above his head, his tiny face pressed against the glass. His face lit up when I raised my thumb and sure enough, the next time I looked across, he had been joined by two others. On my next pass, three became five and before long it was standing room only, as the entire window was lined with infant spectators.

I was often grateful when clients were not at home. That way I could just get on with the job without the pressure of being supervised or timed, but this was a whole different ball game. By now, a dozen potential critics lined the circuit. Shielded by panes of glass, they looked like they were all housed in a corporate box and I wish I could have done something more spectacular to amuse them. Even so it seemed the combination of noise and motion was entertainment enough, as I managed to hold their attention for the duration of the job. I could have sold tickets.

Conscious of the time, I waved goodbye to the kids, loaded everything onto the vehicle and drove off, as I had an appointment with a fellow called John Smalls, a local estate agent.

John's firm had been appointed by Sir Ronald and Lady Norman, owners of the St. Clere Estate (a massive property about fifteen minutes drive from Sevenoaks), to find a suitable tenant for a recently renovated office unit on their property. The unit – 4 Lakeview Stables, was one of five that had once formed a cluster of farm buildings.

John had emailed me a brochure a few days before and as far as I could see the unit was well located, it was the right size and no more expensive than a couple of others (in much less desirable locations), that I had considered.

Following a set of written instructions and a map, I drove into the estate (admiring the magnificent four storey mansion on top of the hill) and followed the signs to Lakeview Stables. The office complex was indeed next to a magnificent lake and though completely refurbished, it had retained its original layout, structure and charm.

My commute from Sevenoaks had taken me through the village of Seal and onto Watery Lane, a winding, picture post card, country road. The drive to the office was glorious and St. Clere itself looked like a film set, which on occasion it was. Most famously for a film adapted from the Agatha Christie novel 'The Mirror Crak'd,' starring Rock Hudson and Elizabeth Taylor.

John was waiting for me as I arrived and I am willing to bet he has never closed a deal as quickly as he did that day. Unit 4 was a single storey office with four allocated parking spaces. It was rectangular in shape, had its original rustic timber beams exposed, plenty of natural light, a kitchenette and bathroom. It was a unique facility in an extraordinary location. I thought it was perfect and pending Jason's approval (upon his return to the UK) we would take it.

The fact that I managed to enlist a new client while I was there was something of a bonus.

Gladys Wood lived in a small cottage that adjoined Unit 4. She had worked as a housekeeper at St. Clere for most of her life and was rewarded in her retirement with a quaint and delightful abode, complete with a small, picturesque garden.

She tended to the flower beds herself and grew a few vegetables in a greenhouse but there were two or three medium size trees that were getting a little out of hand and she asked me if I knew how to prune them.

Of course I said that I did (having made such a spectacular success of Stephanie Beattie's Wisteria) and believing that I would find sufficient reference in 'Pruning,' agreed to return later that week to tackle the job.

I had bought a set of long handle 'loppers' from Godfrey's (which helped to make light work of jobs such as this) and got stuck in with (I fear) a little too much gusto. I cut off one branch, then another, which set something of a precedent and before I knew it I had pruned one entire side of the tree pretty much back to the trunk.

It looked a bit severe but I had no choice other than to prune the other side in a similar fashion, as any other approach would be an admission of error. As I did however, my heart began to sink. What (minutes before) had been a healthy and robust tree, now resembled more of a small totem pole. Worse still, Gladys had just opened the front door and she was now walking towards me in order to make an initial inspection.

I panicked, but then decided that the best form of defence was attack and I greeted her like a long lost friend.

'Mrs Wood!' I said enthusiastically, 'I'm really pleased you're here, so I can show you what I've done.'

I explained how concerned I was that the tree I was pruning was located quite close to the clothes' line and that in its former guise, it really was quite dangerous. After all, it only takes a second to lose an eye. In any case, I had pruned it back quite heavily (apparently) to stimulate a new and more robust growth spurt and that what looked quite harsh now would in fact pay dividends down the track with a rich and full foliage.

I had almost managed to convince myself at that stage and stood there nervously waiting for her to respond.

Gladys (bless her) looked at the 'tree' and nodded her head, saying 'Yes, okay. Well I can see you know what you are doing.'

CHAPTER 13

THE SEVENOAKS TSUNAMI

I have long been fascinated by the incredible diversity of accents in the United Kingdom. It is possible to travel only a few miles and find people speaking quite differently. Some accents are quite easy on the ear, while others (such as those emanating from Birmingham) are not.

I quite like the Yorkshire accent for example. At least, I quite liked Alison Kirkbright's Yorkshire accent anyway. Alison lived in Chipstead but she was originally from 'The North.' She was friendly, attractive and the mother of three children. One of whom was a devoted Leeds United fan – poor fellow.

To this day, I am not certain just where 'The North' begins (or ends) but those who are from 'it,' seem quite proud to be so. I have never known anyone to boast they are from 'The South' for example.

Alison became a semi-regular client, which meant I was

generally called upon to mow the lawns when her own children had either refused or made a mess of it and to trim a conifer hedge that divided her front garden from a neighbour's driveway.

Chatting with her was like going away for the weekend. She was always friendly and I often entertained myself (while mowing) by mimicking some of her phrases and expressions.

'I would make cuppa tea but husband's got electric off' was a particular favourite, as was 'I saw her other day in street, walking dog.'

When I first met her, she drove a burgundy coloured people carrier - a vehicle that was perhaps a little bit of 'The North' transplanted in the South East. Regrettably that didn't last and it was replaced by a silver Land Rover, something more befitting the Sevenoaks stereotype. Pity.

Paula Wilks by comparison, drove a navy blue Renault Espace the whole time that I knew her. Respect. She was originally from Wales and lived in Woodside Road.

One of the very first people to have received a Jim's Mowing leaflet, she was actually at home when I delivered it and confessed to making sure the door was locked when she saw me coming down the drive. Luckily, she found the time to surf across the Australian web site and was encouraged by the fact there was a substantial organisation behind the circus animal making its way up the street.

Every 'Jim' should have a client like Paula Wilks. I referred to her property as the 'Woodside Tea Rooms,' given every time I arrived there (to do anything), she would produce cups of coffee, freshly baked muffins, cakes, cookies and bars of chocolate - even if I was working next door.

I mowed Paula's lawn every fortnight. I put up fences and trellis, landscaped the back corner of her garden, planted a few trees and generally did whatever tasks sprang to mind. How I didn't put on a stone remains a mystery.

One day I pulled a few weeds from her children's vegetable garden and was presented with a 'cheque' by her four year old son. It was a series of doodles scribbled on a Post It note with a figure vaguely resembling a two. I thought it was a very generous payment for less than a minute's work and to this day, I haven't had the heart to bank it.

Carina Gustavsson completed my World Cup Trifecta. She was beautiful, Swedish and lived in Bayham Road. If Carina didn't win the Sevenoaks 'best dressed' title year on year, she was a cinch to finish in the top ten. Whether she was hitting the golf course, going out to lunch or just hanging around the house, she always looked immaculate, which made for an interesting contrast with my grass stained uniform and muddy boots.

I tended to her lawns every fortnight and was called upon to do pretty much all there was to do outside. I trimmed the hedges, dismantled an old green house, pressure washed the paving, decking and outdoor furniture.

One day she asked me to clean the roof of the car port. The roof itself was little more than a number of clear plastic sheets attached to a timber frame, and as it was essentially flat and sitting directly underneath a large pine tree, it was sagging beneath a weight of needles, twigs, water and moss.

Carina accepted my quote to clear it all away and I returned early the next day to find that frost and ice had been added to the equation overnight.

I had no intention of getting up there, as one slip would surely see me crashing through and onto the roof of a fully optioned Land Rover Sport.

Instead, I set a ladder against one side of the car port and fixed a wide broom head to an extension pole. That way I didn't have to actually get up on the roof, yet I could still reach across its entire width to gather all of the mess.

It seemed like the perfect plan.

I climbed up the ladder, to a height where my waist was just below the level of the roof and launched the pole across. As luck would have it, the width of the broom sat perfectly within the confines of each plastic sheet, so I was able to gain a generous purchase on all the muck and at the same time, contain it within a single, narrow channel.

I drew the pole towards me, pulling as hard as I could, not realising a number of things. Firstly, there was more water, ice and muck gathered there than I had first thought. Secondly it was freezing cold and third, I had no realistic means of escape.

I was perched several rungs up (at what I considered to be 'ankle breaking height' should I decide to jump), watching a gathering tsunami of ice, moss and pine needles rolling towards me. It was like wading into the breakers at Portsea in mid winter, as a filthy, icy torrent flooded my trousers.

My body froze and my heart raced, as I let rip with a breathless scream. It felt like I was being stabbed by hundreds of tiny ice daggers, as the filthy surge ran down my legs and flooded my boots. I clung to the ladder, shaking and shivering, all the while cursing the abominable English climate.

I managed to climb down and fearing hypothermia might set in any second, ripped off my boots, wrung out my socks and ran barefoot back to the truck. It was a five minute drive back to my flat, where after a quick bath and a change of clothes, I returned to the fray.

From there, I drove to Nicola Gill's new place. She had recently moved (only a few miles) from 'The Nearly Corner Oast' to 'The Little House' in Stone Street.

Either the bloke who built the place was called 'Little,' or it was someone's idea of a joke, as no reasonable person could possibly describe any aspect of her new property in such modest terms.

The house itself was big and the surrounding property (which incorporated an orchard) huge. It had a large lawn at the front and an even bigger one alongside. There was a patch of grass surrounded by a conifer hedge (I reckon it was once a tennis court), some steep banks that would have to be strimmed and grass just about as far as the eye could see.

I had always refused the opportunity to invest in a ride on mower, as living in a flat, I didn't have a realistic means of storing one. By the same token, tackling 'The Little House' with my twenty one inch Honda would be a full time job in itself, as by the time I had finished strimming and mowing, I dare say the grass that I had first cut would have already grown back.

I suggested to Nicola that I could get her a good deal on a 'ride on' at Godfrey's. She agreed and the following week I was back in the saddle of her brand new John Deere. I scheduled the job for every second Friday afternoon. That way I might stagger home exhausted but have the weekend to look forward to.

The whole job took about four and half hours to complete and I was often impressed and grateful that Nicola went to such lengths and travelled such distances, just to bring me a cup of tea.

Her two sons returning home from school added an additional health and safety dimension to the exercise, as Toby (in particular) enjoyed following me around on his bicycle and I certainly didn't fancy explaining a collision to his mother.

One day he and his younger brother Lucas were tearing around, just as I was clearing the last few clippings and leaves from the driveway, when I cheekily blasted him in the face with a shot from the blower. He laughed, thought it was a great lark and asked me to do it again. I thought it was a bit rude to leave his brother out of the loop, so I gave Lucas a serve as well. Suffice to say, he felt rather differently. At first, he didn't react at all and it looked to me, as though he was collecting his thoughts, before embarking on a course of action. Then his bottom lip started to quiver and I could see tears welling up in his eyes. At this point, I could see I was in trouble and I suggested that perhaps Toby might like to step in. Being older (I think he was about seven) he wasn't the least bit concerned and assured me that his little brother was 'always doing that.'

I looked back to see Lucas was now in full cry and worse still, he was heading back to the house, to the sanctuary and comfort of his mother's arms.

I felt sure I was just minutes away from being sacked and I pleaded with Toby to intervene, but he just hopped on his bike and rode away.

I weighed up the options and decided that trying to explain and apologise to Nicola (and Lucas) didn't really appeal, so I loaded up the van and left.

If anything was to come of it, I would just tell her his brother did it.

CHAPTER 14

THE ULTIMATE UPPER BODY WORKOUT

The entrance to Montreal Road looked just like any other on the Sevenoaks landscape, tucked away as it was, just beyond the roundabout at Riverhead. Yet the road itself was once a very grand driveway that led to a magnificent stately home. No remnants of the old mansion remained but judging by the size of the Oak trees that lined the street it must have been quite something in its day.

Once the original house had been demolished, the grounds were redeveloped as a residential estate. Dozens of two storey houses were built on large blocks, all in the same style and all bordered by Beech hedges. Curiously, every single property in Montreal Road had a name. God forbid that its residents would have to tolerate anything so common as numbers.

Mr Dorban lived at 'Hill Stone.' He had been referred by a friend and needed someone to trim the hedge at the front of his property, as 'the fellow who normally does it has hurt his shoulder.'

Apparently it was 'that time of year again' when the hedges had to be trimmed and Mr Dorban suggested that if I could make a good fist of it, his friend and neighbour across the street would be interested in having his done as well.

I hadn't tackled a Beech hedge before and I wasn't too sure just how far back it should be cut, so I set about it slowly and carefully. As it happens, Mr Dorban turned out to be a pretty good coach. At one point he took hold of the hedge trimmer and ran a couple of swipes for me, expertly angling the blades to achieve a neater, smoother finish than I had been able to achieve to that point.

It took me three goes but it eventually passed inspection and a couple of days later I was giving the hedges at 'Cawdries' a similar treatment across the road.

By the time I completed that job, I had been asked to quote two others.

I had plenty of other work booked in and was having trouble getting out of Montreal Road at all, as each job I secured seemed to lead to another. I dealt with Mrs McIntyre at 'Bend Oak' and spent an entire day working for Stewart McLaren at 'Sandmount West,' before Mr Todd from 'The Robyns' asked me to trim all of his hedges - front, back and sides.

Having seen and trimmed enough hedges to last a lifetime, my interest and enthusiasm was fading and I am the first to admit that I didn't do a particularly good job at 'The Robyns' - at least not the first time around anyway. I finished the hedges, shoved an invoice through the door and took a call from Mr Todd that night. He wasn't happy with the job I had done and asked me to come back and finish it off before he would pay me. I was tired, angry and thought my arms were about to fall off but I returned early the next day, insisting there couldn't possibly be anything wrong with it.

Mr Todd had the advantage of being able to survey the site from an upstairs window, so I set my ladder up to replicate his view as best I could. I managed to perch myself both high and far enough away to see over the top and I had to admit he was right. The hedges I had trimmed looked a scale model of the Sussex Downs. They were indeed bumpy and uneven, to say nothing of the fact that several twigs and shoots were sticking up indiscriminately.

I gave each one another pass with the hedge trimmer and once satisfied they were straight and even, I left a note and packed everything onto the van.

Just as I was about to leave I was collared by a neighbour - a South African IT consultant who worked from home. He lived at 'Absolute Wanker' – at least that's what it says in the diary.

Needless to say, his property was surrounded by Beech hedges. I took an instant dislike to him and added an 'aggravation element' to my quote, which he had the temerity to accept. I carried on with the job then and there, which he personally supervised throughout, pointing out minor errors and oversights, insisting they were corrected immediately.

He wandered in and out of the house a few times and at one point, returned drinking tea and eating biscuits – neither of which he offered me. It was the closest I ever came to walking away from a job.

Even so, Montreal Road was proving to be the ultimate upper body workout. After wielding a petrol driven, hedge trimmer attachment for hours on end, to say nothing of raking mountains of clippings and hurling them into the back of the truck, it was little wonder I had shoulders like an East German breast stroker. That night, I slouched in the bath, fearing that I had contracted some horrible disease, such was the bulging muscle definition in my forearms.

My last Beech hedge trim was for Mrs Forster who lived at 'Glenwood,' right on the bend of the road. From the front of her property, I could see to the other end of the street and straight ahead was the entrance to Montreal Road itself. It was like a light at the end of the tunnel.

Her front hedge wasn't too big or too bad and I managed to get it trimmed and tidied in about an hour. The property was quite long and narrow however, with Beech and Conifer hedges running the entire length of the back garden on both sides.

I worked my way down the left, negotiating a path through the flower beds, raking out as many of the clippings as I could, when Mrs Forster wandered outside and presented me with a cheque. She thanked me for doing such a good job and explained that as she had to take her daughter to a dancing class, she wouldn't be back at all that day. I thanked her very much, wished her all the best and started eyeing off the trampoline that was sitting in the middle of the lawn.

I had worked in several gardens that housed trampolines and had never considered having a go myself, but for some reason I was inextricably drawn to this one. Aside from the fact my client wasn't at home and would not be coming back for some time, I think perhaps the lure was a desire to celebrate the end of the Montreal Road hedge trimming season.

Once I had finished the hedges on the other side, raked up the clippings and blown the last few shreds next door, I loaded everything on to the vehicle and returned to the back garden.

Mrs Forster's car was no longer in the drive, there were no lights on in the house and I doubt any of the neighbours could see, much less care, so I whipped off my boots and jumped aboard.

My first few forays were nervous and clumsy, but I soon found my timing and before long I was happily bouncing to a decent height.

It was time to turn a few tricks.

Given I was breaking a twenty year trampolining drought, I wasn't overly confident that I could pull off even the most basic manoeuvre and decided to provide myself with a boisterous commentary as a means of motivation.

According to my deluded fantasy, I was one simple

execution away from victory in the World Championships and convinced that millions were watching, glued to television sets around the globe.

I bounced up and down a few times, building the tension to a fever pitch, before stretching my legs in front of me, landing on my backside and bouncing up again. I managed to straighten my legs on the descent, just enough to stay upright and maintain enough elevation to continue.

The crowd went absolutely mad and the title was mine. I raised both arms in the air, declared myself to be 'an absolute bloody champion!' and then caught sight of two young girls standing just outside the back door of the house. They were both carrying small rucksacks and dressed in school uniform - I dare say Mrs Forster's elder daughter and a friend. They looked like matching book ends, as they stood side by side, with their jaws dropped and mouths wide open.

It took me at least three or four bounds before I could come to halt. I climbed down, pulled on my boots and proceeded to inspect the frame of the trampoline, confirming that the platform was indeed secure and level. I tapped the edge of the mat firmly, said aloud 'Yeah, that'll hold alright!' and walked out.

CHAPTER 15

LOWERING THE TONE

I was all too often surprised and disappointed, when some British people that I met said they couldn't understand why I would want to live and work in the UK, in preference to somewhere like Australia. Notwithstanding the fact it was always my intention to return home one day, I thought it was a shame that they didn't seem to appreciate much of what they had.

Winter was approaching by the time Jason was due to return to the UK. The days were getting shorter but the West Kent landscape was rendered all the more spectacular as a consequence. Exploring some of the narrow, tree lined lanes that surround Sevenoaks was an absolute joy and when the sun did shine, it made for a glorious festival of warmth and colour.

One day I went for a walk a few minutes from my flat and discovered an old wooden door set in a high stone wall that surrounded the National Trust property of Knole

Park. I couldn't be sure it wasn't a private property but the door was ajar so I opened it and wandered through. Not fifty yards ahead of me, I could see a small herd of spotted deer, quietly grazing at the side of a public footpath. There wasn't another human being in sight, I was ten minutes from home and could be in London (by train) in half an hour.

The next day I did battle with the M25, drove to Heathrow and collected Jason. He intended staying in the UK for about six weeks before flying home for Christmas and returning in January. I certainly didn't envy him the air miles.

A couple of days later, I introduced Jason to Bob Lovitt who prepared and filed all the necessary documentation to enable Jim's Home Services Limited to incorporate in the UK. We hadn't managed to enlist as much shareholder investment as we had originally hoped, but importantly we had a company, a presence and a plan.

I was particularly anxious for Jason to see the office at St. Clere and described it in quite glowing terms to both he and Bob, assuring them that it was 'a hundred times better and yet no more expensive than some pokey little office above a shop in the High Street.' I could have perhaps chosen a more appropriate comparison, given we were sitting in Bob's pokey little office above a shop in the High Street at the time, but happily he didn't appear to take any offence.

Jason agreed that 4 Lakeview Stables was indeed an ideal location and we offered to sign a three year lease. All of the parties seemed perfectly happy with the arrangement but once a couple of solicitors got involved, it proved to be a more drawn out and protracted process than we had hoped.

Jason modelled the Jim's Mowing UK web site on the Australian version and we subscribed to a couple of franchise 'match making sites.' Jason's experience in compiling all of the elements in our information pack was proving invaluable, to say nothing of his experience in recruiting franchisees.

Our first serious enquiry was actually referred to us by Jim's Group in New Zealand. Tim Godden was working as a production manager for a UK packaging firm and was in search of a complete lifestyle change. In fact he and his wife were seriously considering emigrating. As luck would have it, he lived in Rochester - which wasn't all that far away from me in Kent and I was impressed (even a little intimidated), that he seemed to know as much about the Jim's Mowing opportunity, system and structure as me.

Tim had certainly done his research and was well advanced with his application for the appropriate permits and Visas, but as he would actually be 'self employed,' he had hit a bit of a snag with the New Zealand bureaucracy and the whole process had stalled.

By the same token, he had no idea that Jim's was actually in the process of launching in the UK and the prospect of coming on board with us (as our very first franchisee) seemed to excite him no end. We spoke at length on the phone and I think he did a better job of extolling the virtues of a Jim's franchise than I could have. I only wish I had taken a few notes.

We arranged a meeting with Jason at my flat and I was pleased that Tim wasn't put off by the domestic environment. In fact, I think if we had presented him with a contract there and then he probably would have signed it. Instead we followed procedure and arranged for him to spend a couple of days 'in the field,' so that he could get a genuine insight into the business.

I really enjoyed working with Tim. He was very enthusiastic, hard working and good fun. There was probably more that he could teach me than I him (from a practical perspective anyway), but I am sure he found it a worthwhile exercise, even if Nasty Mrs Phillips did berate for us for conducting a 'Mothers' Meeting' on her back lawn.

I introduced Tim to my vehicle and assured him that (despite its rather battered appearance) it was in fact almost new. He seemed quite impressed by its concept and design and I explained that even though the business in Australia had been built on the back of thousands of 'trailers,' I didn't think that they were a realistic option in the UK. Given Rochester was one of the more densely populated parts of Kent, it wasn't something he was ever likely to dispute.

Tim took a copy of the contract with him, giving every indication that he would sign it, as Jason and I were busily making preparations to attend a franchise exhibition at Kensington, Olympia.

The exhibition was effectively the same show that I had attended at Wembley the year before and I hoped that this incarnation would prove to be more productive and enjoyable.

We had a small corner site that was dressed with a couple of banners we had adapted from Australia and a few pieces of equipment that we managed to borrow from Godfrey's. It wasn't the most spectacular stand but it was far from the worst.

We stood there for the best part of two days, meeting and greeting those passing by and handing out information brochures and business cards.

It was enlightening to see the vast range of franchise opportunities on offer. A number of lawn treatment companies were exhibiting, as were various cleaners and printers but I couldn't see anything that was comparable to Jim's.

We did our best to enlist some interest and gathered about fifty names and addresses of people who had asked for more information. As it happens, the most promising enquiry that came from the exhibition was forwarded the next day. It was from a fellow who had seen my vehicle in the car park but hadn't managed to locate our stand. I thought if we did decide to exhibit again, we might just park outside and save ourselves a small fortune.

Returning to Sevenoaks, I attended to my regular clients while Jason did the rounds of the local estate agents, looking to rent a house that would accommodate his wife and twin two year old boys, who would be coming over from Australia in the New Year. Within a couple of weeks, he managed to find a house in Eynsford, which was a fifteen minute drive north of Sevenoaks and about the same distance to the new office.

Jason's move to Eynsford more or less coincided with us taking possession of the office and given Tim Godden had kept in touch, it was exciting to see things starting to take shape. We even had an additional car park constructed for us (by the people at St. Clere) who were concerned that my vehicle might 'lower the tone,' should it be parked within the confines of the Lakeview Stables complex itself.

We had the phones and internet connected, while we installed desks, computers, printers and a meeting table. Sticking a big Jim's Mowing logo on the door completed the baptism, at which point we locked everything up and made a road trip to Leeds and York.

Jim had appointed the Franchise Support Centre (in York) to handle the bulk of our franchise enquiries and job leads and they had sent us what seemed a genuine enquiry from an address in Leeds.

I was looking forward to the trip, as it was an opportunity to meet our new colleagues and we thought the Leeds enquiry sounded quite promising, given the people we had arranged to meet already operated a successful landscaping business.

It was pretty deflating to drive for five hours up the M1, only to find the Leeds address didn't exist, there was no answer on the phone number we had been given and the exercise was nothing more than a hoax. As if to add insult to injury, someone tapped on the window and asked me to present him a quote to trim a hedge. I said that I would love to help, but given I didn't have a single piece of equipment on board and had just driven from Kent, it probably wasn't the best time.

CHAPTER 16

MARKETING

I was gradually building a base of regular clients but chose to continue supplementing my income by working weekends at a couple of Farmers' Markets in London.

On Saturdays I worked at Twickenham, selling all manner of tomatoes that had been grown in poly tunnels and greenhouses on the Isle of Wight and on Sundays I barbecued Lamb Burgers at Islington.

The Twickenham market was set up in a car park, just behind the Marks and Spencer store in the High Street.

Every Saturday morning, a couple of farm employees would load dozens of tomato laden plastic crates onto transit vans, before catching the ferry across to Portsmouth and dropping individual batches off at various market locations in and around London.

I aimed to arrive before 9.00am (M25 willing) which gave me enough time to assemble an interlocking metal stand that was packed in a heavy vinyl sack and left sitting under a tree with all of the day's stock. It was like playing with a giant Meccano set and it generally took me a couple of goes to master its assembly. Once it was intact and standing, I laid four plywood boards over the top and they in turn were dressed with a couple of rolls of artificial grass.

As a rule, I built a mountain of hefty Beefsteaks to my right. Next to them was a tangled pile of Campari vines, then several punnets of Cherries and Santas, bordered by Aranca vines and various tubs, bottles and jars containing all manner of tomato based sauces and toppings.

It was quite a colourful display and I took no small measure of pride in its presentation, even if my sales technique and general attitude was a little more irreverent.

For the most part, the market was populated by genuine farmers, many of whom had travelled from as far away as Lincolnshire and Somerset. I (by comparison) was a complete fraud but the politically correct stance (stipulated by the market management) was to purvey the myth that I worked all week on the farm, that I had been up very early to catch the ferry and under no circumstances had I driven from Kent.

Customers often asked me 'How was the crossing?' with some recalling childhood holidays and their own trips to the island. Having never set foot on the place it was a challenging bluff to maintain and as much as I managed to pull it off most weeks, I did think it was best to 'come clean' once or twice, when I was really pressed.

The tomatoes themselves were delicious and

consequently very popular. Most weeks the time simply flew by, as I busily emptied punnets and vines into paper bags, re-stocking the display, as and when an opportunity presented itself.

It was a social outing as much as a weekend job and I made a lot of friends with customers and stall holders alike. Foremost among them was an eight year 'tom boy' called Lottie. She came to the market most weeks (if she wasn't playing football for the local under tens) and would wave furiously from the front seat of the car, as her mother searched for a parking spot.

She wasn't the least bit shy and had as much charm, character and assertiveness as anyone I have ever met. Lottie is my long range tip for UN Secretary General.

When I first met her, I told her that I was an Australian and asked if she knew where that country was. She most certainly did, whereupon (kneeling down to her height) I added 'I'm from Melbourne.' She wasn't the least bit impressed and looked quite nonplussed. 'Never heard of it' she said.

A succession of eastern Europeans looked after the bread stall to my left and a large and pretentious organic fruit and vegetable operation set up on my right.

Occasionally the market manager squeezed a visiting goat cheese vendor between us. Goat Man presented his wares dressed like a lab technician and when I made the mistake of remarking that I didn't realise the process of making his cheese was such a science, he swiftly corrected me.

'Actually, it's more of an art' he said indignantly.

I didn't bother speaking to him again.

Piers set up opposite me most weeks, selling Buffalo meat, mozzarella and yoghurt. He was what a lot of British people describe as a 'nutter.' He had waist length hair tied back in a pony tail, he wore shorts year round, supported Chelsea with a passion and could talk under water with a mouth full of marbles. People thought he was either a great character (as did I, for the most part anyway), or an absolute pain in the neck. A rather dry witted Irish customer of mine summed him up (for many) one day, when he said that Piers was living proof of the widely held theory, that 'under every pony tail is a horse's arse.'

I really enjoyed working at Twickenham, as most of my customers were very pleasant, friendly and regular. It was rare that anyone suffered my zero tolerance policy when it came to rudeness or complaints about prices.

I started chatting to a fellow one day who asked me what I did for a job when I wasn't selling tomatoes. I was too busy to try and explain the whole Jim's Mowing franchising thing, so I opted to tell him of my secondary vocation and said that I was writing a book. He nodded approvingly and returned a few minutes later when the rush had died down a bit.

'I have thought of a publisher who would be interested in your book.' he said.

'Really?!' I said excitedly, thinking that I might soon launch myself from weekend tomato vendor into the realms of the literary elite.

'Yes!' he said 'the Lord Jesus Christ.'

Suffice to say, I was a little disappointed and questioned the amount of any advance I was likely to negotiate with his 'publisher.'

'The best advance you could ever hope for!' he said 'forgiveness for all your sins!'

I said 'Thanks very much, but if it's all the same to him, I would just as soon have the cash.'

I worked at Twickenham for a couple of years and given the seasonal nature of the produce, managed to have the winters off. The market was like a cashless economy, as each week I left with a car load of vegetables, bread and cheese, all bartered for by exchanging an excess stock of tomatoes.

My Sunday job was in Islington – a part of North London that had recently transformed itself from run down and rough to trendy and desirable.

Most of the customers who attended each week were representative of its more recent incarnation with the odd B-List celebrity thrown in.

My employer was Mary, an eccentric sheep farmer from Battle in Sussex. She lived and worked alone, was grossly overweight and a larger than life character.

Mary drove a battered old Subaru, towing a small livestock trailer that was weighed down with a heavy gas barbecue, a dozen or so 'cool boxes' full of meat, three or four plastic tables, a couple of umbrellas and assorted junk.

The market itself was set up in a courtyard opposite Islington Green and at the end of a narrow lane that housed a number of small antique shops. Twenty odd stalls were packed into a small space and at peak times it was very crowded. I was banished to the fringes, which made sense given the smoke and fumes the barbecue generated. All the same it worked quite well, as I was able to service the passing trade, as much as the market's own customers, even if I was exposed to the elements.

I caught the train to London Bridge most weeks but scored a lift from Mary early one Sunday morning. She had lost her electricity supply overnight and as a consequence she hadn't been able to mince any of the shoulder joints that she used for the burgers. It was a minor crisis and she asked if we could execute the process at my flat on her way to the market.

It was just before 8.00am when I could be seen carrying several clear plastic bags stuffed with raw meat into 'Ferndale' - the building that housed my flat. A generous trail of blood ran along the footpath and regrettably all over the carpet and stairs. I had already incurred the wrath of my neighbours, after traipsing mud and grass clippings through the foyer but this was something else again. With each pass, I dreaded being accosted by Barbara - my erstwhile nemesis in flat number one. She was the Godmother of the 'Ferndale Mafia' and had made a point of asking me to 'please' preserve the building's new carpet only a few weeks before.

Mary and I must have looked like a couple of serial killers, desperately trying to dispose of a body and even though we managed to escape unnoticed and unscathed, I half expected the Flying Squad to break down the door any second. Suffice to say, I think the entire episode was a damning indictment of the Sevenoaks Neighbourhood Watch programme.

Once we had arrived, unloaded and the barbecue was on its feet, I would scoop up fistfuls off mince, shaping them into neatly pressed burgers, all arranged and stacked on white plastic trays. Bread rolls were cut in half, shoved in plastic bags and baskets, while Mary laid on an array of sauces and condiments. The market opened at 10.00am and most days we were busy from the outset and manic around lunchtime. Mary usually managed to sell out of all but a few sausages within an hour or two, at which point she was able to press more burgers and cut more bread rolls to help fuel the Lamb Burger juggernaut.

People queued up to twenty at a time and we kept a hectic pace, sharing the same indifference to those who enquired as to whether the meat was organic and often complimented each other on our thinly veiled barbs in reply.

I heard one terribly proper woman ask Mary one day 'How are your joints?'

'Mine all ache' she said.

There was more of a community feel amongst the market traders at Islington. That may have been down to the fact that each week we were huddled quite close together but I reckon it had more to do with the fact the Camden Head was right next door. Many of us adjourned there each week after the market had closed, while one or two would partake of its wares a little earlier.

Each week Les could be seen nursing a pint of Guinness on his stall (just as soon as the pub opened) while he worked his way through the Times Crossword, in between sales of Pheasant and Duck.

'Hey burger boy!' he called out one day. 'Slang for Aussie farmer?! Five letters!'

Islington was good fun. The market had a friendly and relaxed vibe about it and I could eat all that I could for free. As at Twickenham I had made some good friends but it was hard work and I found myself getting home quite late. After my obligatory Sunday night Chinese take away, I would often fall asleep on the couch and start the working week feeling tired. It was time to leave the markets and focus on the bigger picture.

CHAPTER 17

WELL, IT SEEMED LIKE A GOOD IDEA AT THE TIME

I came to regret putting an ad in the West Kent Yellow Pages. Not so much because it was expensive (which it was) but because I lived more or less on the boundary of its distribution and most of the leads it generated were too far flung to even contemplate.

One worthwhile lead that I did secure however was in a village called Larkfield, which was less than half an hour away. Julie Clarke lived in New Hythe Lane, quite a busy road and one that housed the offices of a number of local businesses. She and her husband wanted to give their front and back gardens a makeover, as they planned to put their house on the market in the spring.

They asked for the front garden beds to be cleaned out, turned over and dressed with bark chips. I should also put down a membrane to stop the weeds coming back and pressure wash the driveway and patio.

There was more to do out the back. A row of dead conifers had to be cut down and dug out, piles of rubbish removed and a whole section of lawn dug out and re-turfed.

I wandered around the garden making notes, drawing diagrams and taking measurements, as snow began to fall. By the time I had finished it was snowing quite heavily and I explained to Julie that I would have to go away, source some materials, and drop a quote in to her in the next couple of days.

It was snowing when I returned two days later and had barely let up in the interim. I knocked on the door, said hello and presented her with my quote. She thought it was 'a bit high' and said she would have to speak with her husband before making a decision. I said that I thought that was perfectly reasonable, just as she alerted me to the fact that none of the other gardeners she had contacted had yet bothered to show up, let alone provide her with a quote.

I seized the opportunity and offered to get started on the job there and then.

'But it's snowing,' she said.

'She'll be right,' I replied, suggesting that I could get most of the hack work done today and return tomorrow with the turf, bark and pressure washer.

She seemed impressed with my enthusiasm and told me to go ahead. I thought it was a great result and I was actually looking forward to working in the snow. I gathered a few tools from the truck and started digging out the weeds in the front garden, as a thick white blanket gathered around me.

The novelty wore off after about fifteen minutes. By then, my gloves and boots were sopping wet, I could barely feel my fingers and I certainly wasn't having any fun. To make matters worse it was now snowing even more heavily than before. I resorted to working in relatively short bursts, ducking under the front verandah every few minutes, ripping off my gloves and furiously rubbing my hands together. I hated having to put them back on but figured cold is fleeting, while blisters last. Even so, I was determined not to be defeated by the weather and kept working at a furious pace.

I weeded the front beds as if my life depended on it, cut down the dead conifer shrubs, dug out the stumps and threw all of the rubbish in the back of the truck. After rewarding myself with a hearty serving of Fish 'n' Chips for lunch, I returned to the fray, skimming the top off what lawn there was with a shovel and turning over the ground with a fork. I then carefully raked over the soil and called it a day, just as it was getting dark.

It didn't appear to have snowed much overnight but it was still bitterly cold the next morning. I called by Richard Abel's and dumped a tonne bag of bark chips in the truck, together with several metres of turf and made my way over to Larkfield.

I thought it best to work from back to front. Lay the turf on the back lawn and then spread the bark chips on the front garden. That way I could finish off and clean up with the pressure washer.

It was a simple enough plan but I hadn't counted on the fact that the soil I had forked and raked the previous day would be frozen solid. Rather than finding an even surface of lush top soil, I was confronted with a mass of frozen grey clumps that looked like a bunch of icy golf balls sitting in a bunker. I couldn't possibly lay the turf over them and to make matters worse, what little sun there was would be shielded from that section of the lawn, owing to a shadow cast by the house. Consequently, it was unlikely to thaw for some time and I made a start with the bark out the front in the hope that it would.

An hour later, little had changed and I resorted to raking all the icy balls to one side and thereafter digging down a few inches below the surface. I shovelled the unfrozen soil into a wheelbarrow, raked the frozen clumps into the hole that I had just made and top dressed it with the soil from the barrow. It was tedious, time consuming and potentially ineffective but as far as I was concerned it was working. I rolled out and pressed down each roll of turf, neatly trimming the edges, desperately hoping it would not subside during the spring thaw.

I then drove from Larkfield to Harrison Way in Sevenoaks, where I had a job booked in with one of my regular mowing clients. Miranda was Dutch and she lived on the corner of what was a very narrow crescent. I had been able to park in her driveway in the past but as she would be 'coming and going,' I would have to leave the truck outside.

That was all well and good until a couple of her neighbours felt the need to lean on their car horns, alerting most of the street to the fact they had trouble driving past, whereupon I thought it best to park on the grass verge outside her property.

Miranda had asked me to cut down a number of branches from a large tree that was overhanging the house and prune all of the shrubs and hedges surrounding the lawn.

Garden clean up jobs like hers would invariably accumulate two or three times the amount of waste and clippings that I initially expected and this one was certainly no exception. It was as if every branch, leaf and frond multiplied three fold once it hit the ground. In any case, I raked them all up, piled everything into the back of the truck and after a jumping up and down on it all a few times it was 'off to the tip.'

Or not, as it happened.

One of the features of the Volkswagen Transporter is that it is front wheel drive, which is all well and good if you are poodling around on tarmac but a bit of disaster if all four wheels are parked on a patch of damp grass with a heavy load of garden waste shoved in the back.

I started the motor, engaged first gear, lifted the clutch and spun the front wheels. I tried again with the same outcome. On my third attempt I planted the proverbial 'pedal to the metal' and went precisely nowhere. I was clearly in a bit of a bind and trying to think laterally, I decided I would reverse and swing the vehicle (albeit blindly) out onto the road. Nothing. With the weight in the back lifting the front wheels ever so slightly off the ground and no drive at all emanating from the rear, the tyres just spun and spun.

I jumped out of the cab and studied the situation. After several attempts, I reckon I had managed to move the vehicle about four inches - all of it downwards, as both front tyres had churned up the grass, gouging two deep troughs in Miranda's front lawn.

It was an ugly sight and a depressing situation. I resorted to dragging all the rubbish out of the back and piling it on the lawn, thinking that without the weight there I might be able to extricate myself. I even tried wedging a couple of braches under the front tyres but short of digging up half the lawn I had run out of options.

I rang Volkswagen Roadside Assist and was assured that someone would come by and help me as 'soon as possible.'

I was able to occupy myself in the interim by putting all of the rubbish (once again) into the back of the truck. I also took the time to calculate the amount of top soil and turf I would need to repair the damage and compose a viable explanation as to what I was doing sitting in my vehicle, parked on a client's lawn for hours at a time - should any one ask.

It was pitch black, 8.00pm and over four hours later when I was finally towed off the lawn. Even in that light the damage was obvious, so I forked over the two deep depressions I had created, before returning the following morning with a sack of top soil, a metre of turf and a box of chocolates for Miranda.

Jason arrived back in the UK soon after and I brought him up to speed with some of the franchise enquiries we had generated in his absence. One of those enquiries rang me on my mobile as we were driving back from the airport. It was a fellow called Trevor Middleton who lived in East Sussex.

'I've just seen one of your vehicles on the M25,' he said.

Though he had effectively spotted the entire fleet, I didn't dare correct him.

'Really?' I said 'could be anyone I suppose.'

Trevor had found our listing on a franchise match making web site, he had read through the information we had sent him and he was keen to know more. I made an appointment for Jason and I to meet with him later that week.

In the meantime two other prospects had surfaced.

One was an accountant from Norfolk and the other a sales representative for Coca-Cola in Wiltshire. Both were quite capable gardeners but they contrasted in almost every other respect. The accountant was in his fifties, he had a professional background and was married with two children. The sales rep by comparison was single, twenty five and looked like he should be in school.

Soon after, Jason and I arranged to meet Trevor at his house in Slinfold. Trevor was in his early forties, he was powerfully built and looked like he could handle himself. Something I made a mental note of, lest I spend too much time looking at his girlfriend. I let Jason do all of the talking, as he was vastly more experienced than I when it came to explaining the Jim's franchise structure. I felt a bit like a third wheel but when Trevor alerted us to the fact his current job involved testing commercial aircraft for signs of metal fatigue I was able to chime in.

'Well, you are well located then,' I said. 'Quite close to Gatwick.'

'Yeah,' he replied dryly. 'Pity I work at Heathrow.'

It was some time before I opened my mouth again.

Jason explained the virtues and features of the Jim's system in great detail, but to be fair I think Trevor was pretty much sold on the concept before we had arrived.

Something that struck me while we were there was how much he was looking forward to doing a job for someone that had the simple courtesy to say 'thank you' when he had finished.

I was able to assure him that I was thanked several times a day and often presented with cups of tea, sandwiches, cakes and biscuits, which seemed disproportionately generous in comparison with someone who helped to keep a commercial airliner up in the air.

CHAPTER 18

THE STONE STREET MOLE INVASION

Jason's family entourage arrived in the UK towards the end of February. It consisted of his wife, twin two year old boys and both parents in law. The plan was that they would all stay in the Eynsford house with the in laws heading home after a few weeks.

Jason had been born in the UK and as far as I can recall his wife had never even visited the country. In any case, it probably wasn't the best time of year to arrive - first impressions and all that. I imagine it was hot and sunny in Melbourne when they left and it was anything but when they touched down at Heathrow. It was the middle of winter and consequently cold, wet and dark.

In hindsight, Eynsford probably wasn't the best choice Jason could have made. It is a very pretty village but as parochial as any in the country - the sort of place where one qualifies as 'local' after about three generations. It had a couple of pubs and two shops, one of which sold handmade chocolates and the other was a butcher that sold locally reared meat. The closest supermarket was a fifteen minute drive and it was possible to walk the length of the main street during the day without seeing another soul.

When I first investigated the local property options, I quickly dismissed the surrounding small villages as ghost towns and Eynsford, for all its quaintness and charm would have probably topped the list in that respect. I had never met Jason's family before and to be fair I barely knew him, but I regret not suggesting Sevenoaks as an alternative. Even so, renting a family home in what was reputed to be the most expensive town in England would have made a right mess of the company's finances.

Sadly, it was clear from the outset that Jason's family relocation wasn't going to work out. Having the in laws on hand kept a lid on the problem for a time but things started to go downhill quite quickly, once they returned to Australia.

That issue aside however, the business was progressing. Tim Godden and Trevor Middleton had all committed to spending a week in Australia, to attend the franchisee training course at the Jim's Group head office, while Jason would present the same course himself for Jody Chrich (the kid from Coca Cola) at the office in Kent.

Wherever possible, we encouraged anyone intending to come on board to train in Australia. We could and in time would replicate the course in the UK but we thought that travelling to Melbourne would enable prospective franchisees to see for themselves just how huge and diverse the business had become.

I was by now combining the operation of my own franchise with working in the office and I spent several days showing our prospects the ropes out in the field.

One of my regular clients at the time was a couple who were both doctors and lived on a large property in Stone Street. The job normally entailed a lot of mowing and I had been called upon to complete a few landscaping jobs and general clean ups every so often as well.

With the onset of spring, I noticed that a couple of small mounds of soil had started to appear in the lawn. Two or three, became five or six after a couple of weeks and another fortnight later we were well and truly into double figures. The culprit was a mole. Not a creature I was particularly familiar with but after some internet research, I discovered it was a small rodent like animal that was effectively blind and burrowed its way beneath the surface devouring worms, while it constructed a network of tunnels in the hope of attracting a mate.

Apparently moles were quite common and I was assured that the best way to be rid of them was by means of setting a trap. I spoke with my contacts at the garden centre and bought a device that I can best describe as being like a very large clothes peg. It was a stainless steel contraption and the idea was to set it in the ground beneath one of the mounds. The mole would then burrow through it, trip the spring and be clamped around the neck, until such time as someone (that is to say me) arrived, dug it up and managed to repatriate it to a more suitable environment - which is a polite way of saying smash on the head with a shovel.

The trap was a very simple concept and possessed of a basic construction. It was clearly conceived on the premise that moles are not only blind but apparently stupid and I happily parted with ten pounds having been given every assurance that they in fact were.

I returned to the battleground and surveyed the site, trying to ascertain where best to set the trap. As far as I could see a network of tunnels had been constructed in an entirely random fashion. Thinking the culprit was more likely to travel along one of its newer avenues, I dug under one of the fresh mounds while feeling around for the direction of the tunnel. I wasn't wearing gloves at the time and made a thorough disturbance in order to frighten the beast away, lest it mistook my finger for a giant earthworm.

I set the trap and optimistically returned the next day to inspect it. Nothing had happened. The trap was still set and there were no new mounds in the lawn. To date, a scoreless draw and I vowed to call by and inspect it as often as I could.

Three days later there was no change but a week after that I found a fresh mound of soil less than a foot from the one where I had set the trap in the first place. It was as if the mole had constructed a bypass, specifically to avoid my clumsy contraption. Determined not to be out smarted by a small blind rodent, I dug up the trap and set it again in the fresh mound, while filling in the tunnel beneath the original.

My subsequent inspections only revealed more mounds and no moles. I was losing the battle, and embarked on a simple war of attrition. Rather than invest in more traps or for that matter, keep moving the original one about, I would simply leave it in place and afford the animal the opportunity to do the decent thing. Either that or assume that its tunnel network would eventually reach capacity, whereupon it would simply be a matter of time before mole and trap would coincide.

Regrettably I never got the chance, as my 'mole role' was superseded. I found myself the victim of a modern day industrial revolution, replaced by a high tech device, marketed by some charlatan masquerading as a 'wildlife specialist.'

Apparently the device could be set up in the garden, where it would emit an uncomfortable frequency, a sound that your average mole would find thoroughly ear piercing. The creature would then abandon its tunnel network and probably move next door, generating the prospect of another sale.

Personally, I favoured patience and a shovel.

By the time the Stone Street Mole had won a clear points victory, our first two franchisees had returned from Australia and given Tim accorded more importance to the fact, he would be the first to sign his contract.

He, Jason and I convened at the office one evening where we conducted a ritual that took just over two hours. Tim was tasked with selecting a single post code that would define his territory and which other codes would comprise his 'local' and 'all areas.'

Thereafter we conducted a sign up interview and questionnaire which seemed designed to catch out anyone who might have fallen asleep during the training course. In truth, Tim had to demonstrate that he understood the contract and the extent of his obligations. We then arranged for uniforms, advertising and stationery. Equipment could be sourced from Godfrey's and his vehicle had already been ordered through a Volkswagen dealership in Manchester. Jason signed the contract under a Power of Attorney for Jim, I witnessed and moments later we had a cheque and our very first UK franchisee.

Tim proved a great asset from the outset. His launch meant we soon had a second vehicle on the road in Kent - one that was being driven by someone who was enthusiastic, hard working and capable.

The accountant came on board a couple of weeks later in Norfolk, followed by Jody Chrich in Wiltshire and Trevor Middleton in East Sussex.

Tim in particular was a great help to me. We worked together on a number of jobs and notwithstanding the fact at times I could barely keep up with him, we forged a worthwhile and enjoyable partnership.

Fencing was a particular skill that Tim possessed and one that I was able to benefit from. It enabled us to add another string to each of our respective businesses and where he could count on a reliable labourer, I could boast a skilled craftsman. Putting up fences together was good fun and a good earn, if at times a trifle dangerous. Tim was quite a character and many times he would be holding a post in place while I was wielding a hammer.

'Right' he would say. 'When I nod my 'ead. You 'it it.'

One day we found ourselves installing a number of trellis panels for Paula Wilks at the Woodside Tea Rooms, when her next door neighbour asked us if we could move a fence that bordered the rear of his property. Apparently it had been encroaching on another's land since being reconstructed following the 'Great Storm of 1987.' It was just as well we happened to be working next door that day, otherwise he might have had to wait another eighteen years.

The Great Storm of '87 had been a cataclysmic event in the south east of England in particular. It was immortalised by one particular BBC television weather forecaster who laughed off suggestions (while on air) of an approaching hurricane, reassuring everyone in the country that there was 'absolutely nothing to worry about.' A couple of hours later, as roofs were being torn from houses, trees uprooted and entire communities cut off by flash floods, he was made to look a bit of a dill.

Until October 1987, seven massive Oak trees had bordered the Sevenoaks Vine cricket ground over a hundred years. Six were completely destroyed in the storm, whereupon the local authority chose to plant another seven. These days, visitors to Sevenoaks can stroll amongst the famous 'eight oaks' while watching a game on 'The Vine.'

It's an anomaly that confuses me to this day.

CHAPTER 19

WHEN A TREE FALLS.

Winters were difficult to cope with at the best of times. It was often bitterly cold and losing daylight around four o'clock certainly took some getting used to.

Working in the snow was by now off the agenda altogether and even a quick stroll to the shops on St. John's Hill had to be carefully planned and executed. Snow that fell overnight would often thaw hours later, only to form a thin layer of ice on the footpath the following day. I am convinced this is why penguins have evolved to take such small waddling steps, as executing a lengthy stride on a flat, icy surface could well result in a clumsy back flip and a concussion.

I was always grateful for the fact a pile of local newspapers would appear in the foyer of my building each Thursday, as (if nothing else) they gave me access to the week's television listings.

I never paid much attention to the local news but one

day I did take note of the fact a famous Lime tree, which had been standing in the outfield of the Kent County Cricket Ground at Canterbury, had been uprooted and destroyed in a gale.

It was the lead story on the back page and as a consequence the first article I was likely to read.

The twenty seven metre tree pre-dated the establishment of the ground itself in 1847 and it was believed to have already been some forty years old at that time.

It was certainly a shame but happily the club intended carrying on the tradition and planting another in its place.

More to the point however, there was a paragraph tacked on to the end of the article, alerting readers to the fact that a local cricket association was presenting a series of training courses for aspiring umpires over the course of the winter. Venues included Maidstone, Tunbridge Wells and Sevenoaks and anyone interested should contact a fellow called Ian Fraser on the phone number listed.

As much as I loved the game, I hadn't played for the best part of twenty years and I had never umpired a match in my life. All the same, enrolling might give me a chance to address my burgeoning TV addiction and escape the flat once a week.

I made the call and after a brief chat with Ian, I was on board.

The course was co-ordinated by a handful of members of the Sevenoaks Cricket Umpires and Scorers' Association and presented each week at the local rugby club.

The club itself was a twenty minute walk and my route took me (rather appropriately) across the Sevenoaks Vine cricket ground. Though often covered in snow, it still seemed appropriate to include on my weekly itinerary.

I turned up on the first night and parted with £30 in exchange for a text book, a copy of the MCC Laws of Cricket and a bound copy of the course notes.

The presenters (all veterans of the craft), were dressed as cricket umpires, as they spoke to a dozen or so of us with the aid of a screen, a projector and a Power Point presentation.

The course was presented over ten weeks, covering all forty two of the game's historic and at times complex laws. Those of us who saw it through to the end would have the opportunity to sit an entry level exam, and (all being well) we would then secure an official umpiring qualification.

The atmosphere was warm (even if the room wasn't) and friendly. I was the only Australian, which accorded me novelty status almost immediately, and I felt quite certain I would enjoy myself. And that was despite the fact we were expected to complete a weekly homework assignment.

Each presentation was very thorough and detailed, usually lasting at least two hours, while the homework was comprehensive and marked very harshly, with no shortage of red ink. As a consequence, class numbers gradually dwindled to about four or five after ten weeks.

Having stayed the course, I thought I should at least sit the exam, as if nothing else, I wanted to have something show for all of the time and effort I had devoted.

One of the presenters explained to what remained of the class, that the exam would be held at the HSBC cricket ground in Beckenham. A town in the north-west corner of the county and on the south eastern outskirts of London.

Recognising me as 'from out of town' he addressed me specifically. 'Richard. Do you know where the HSBC ground is in Beckenham?'

I replied that I didn't even know where Beckenham was, which generated a ripple of laughter, before I was presented with a very detailed set of directions that would in fact lead me straight to the ground, assuming I could catch a train to the local station.

On the day in question, I caught the train, made my way to the ground and arrived in plenty of time. I registered and was ushered upstairs into a room which housed fifty or so small desks, arranged in rows facing a large screen and a projector that was suspended from the ceiling.

The exam was presented in a multiple choice format, with a presenter reading a series of sixty questions that were (in turn) displayed on the screen, while each of us was tasked with marking the correct answer (hopefully) on the sheets provided.

I sat in the front row, as the room started to fill, recognising a couple of my Sevenoaks contemporaries amongst an eclectic gathering that must have completed the same training course in other parts of the county.

The questions followed a logical match day sequence,

testing our knowledge of the procedures and processes that umpires should undertake while inspecting the ground, speaking with the captains and executing the toss.

Thereafter, we moved on to various 'No Ball' scenarios, all of which garnered additional concentration, as a single incorrect answer in this sequence alone would result in a fail.

The exam took ninety minutes to complete, while our results would be confirmed by mail in a week or two.

80% was considered a pass (an honours standard in universities) and I was feeling quietly confident afterwards when I was greeted by one of the Sevenoaks contingent, just as I was leaving. I hadn't actually spoken to him before as I think he had only attended some of the classes, but he offered to give me a lift home, which I gratefully accepted.

He too was very confident, as he had been playing the game for several years (most recently for the Sevenoaks second XI). As we drove along he asked me what answer I had given to any number of questions, whereupon it soon became apparent (to me anyway), that one of us had almost certainly failed. I was pretty sure it wasn't me and rather than embarrass my 'lift,' I became rather vague in my recollections and simply responded 'So did I' when he confirmed each answer he had submitted.

It was quite a long trip, as I tried to steer the conversation in a different direction, at least until we reached a point that I could recognise, in the event I should have to walk the rest of the way.

Finally, we reached the outskirts of Sevenoaks and before long I was alighting outside my flat. I thanked my colleague and wished him all the best, in the fervent hope that he did not intend pursuing cricket umpiring as a career.

My results hadn't yet arrived when head tutor John Allen rang to congratulate me. Apparently I had missed a perfect score by just one mark. For what it's worth, umpires (while ultimately responsible for the correctness of the score) are not in fact obliged to confirm it during a drinks break.

John was a delightful man. Calm, friendly and possessed of a very gentle, self deprecating sense of humour, he seemed to have all the qualities a cricket umpire would need and it came as no surprise to learn that he was indeed very well liked and highly respected in the field.

John also managed a panel of umpires that he appointed to various village and school games in and around Kent. I fairly jumped at the chance to join and before long my very first umpiring assignment was confirmed.

I was told that I would stand with an experienced colleague in a pre-season practice match one Sunday at Meopham – a community which boasts the curious title of 'The Longest Village in Britain.'

I invested in the necessary attire – a broad brimmed white hat, white coat, black trousers and white trainers. In addition to bowler's markers, overs cards, a set of bails, a note pad, a couple of clutch pencils (as I didn't trust using a biro in the rain), scissors, band aids and a pocket sized, laminated 'cheat sheet,' detailing some unlikely scenarios and associated penalties should a veritable 'blue mooner' present itself.

Meopham was drawn to play a neighbouring team from New Ifield on the village green. Meopham Green itself was located alongside the A227 and appropriately enough, opposite a pub called The Cricketers' Arms.

I was warmly welcomed into the club's delightful and quaint pavilion, to see various photographs of the Melbourne Cricket Ground adorning the walls. Apparently a touring group of Australian MCC members continue to play a fixture at Meopham during each Ashes tour. It was something John was well aware of and I don't think he could have found a more appropriate venue for me to make my umpiring debut.

I changed in the Umpire's Room at the base of the stairs, before introducing myself to my colleague and the two captains. New Ifield won the toss, chose to bat and we took the field under a clear blue sky.

I chose to stand at the pavilion end and having meticulously inspected the stumps, crease markings and counted the fielders, tossed the ball to the opening bowler. I confirmed the batsman's guard, checked my watch, indicated the bowler's mode of delivery, then took up a position and prepared to launch my umpiring career with the call of 'Play!'

I concentrated heavily, as the bowler approached and

the batsman faced up. As the bowler entered his delivery stride, I carefully focussed on the position of his feet, being sure to move my eyes only and not my head (as we had been taught), so that I could more readily detect just where the ball might pitch, in the event of an appeal for leg before wicket.

I held my breath, prepared for anything, as the batsman let a harmless and perfectly innocuous delivery travel wide of his off stump and through to the wicket keeper.

It was by any measure, spectacularly uneventful.

As the game progressed, I was still feeling quite nervous but enjoying myself immensely and after successfully negotiating the first few overs, found myself presented with my very first 'challenge.'

I was standing at the striker's end (square leg) when the New Ifield captain launched a powerful pull shot, heaving the ball high in the air and directly over my head. I turned around, following the flight of the ball, watching it disappear over the boundary, when I first caught a glimpse of a dark green Jaguar travelling south along the A227.

Even my rudimentary grasp of physics indicated that the descent of the ball and path of the vehicle were almost certain to coincide and sure enough they did with an almighty thud.

My colleague dutifully signalled 'six,' as with a screech of brakes the Jag ground to a halt. The driver got out, inspected the damage and with an angry, purposeful gait, marched straight onto the field, making a bee line for me.

I quickly recounted all of the 42 Laws I had studied, together with the field craft and personnel management solutions we had been taught, but I couldn't recall anything that came under the heading 'Irate motorist invades field of play.'

The driver began protesting the damage to his car just as one of the Meopham players ran over, suggesting he speak to their president, who could explain the process involved in making a claim on the club's insurance. Apparently damage to moving cars was covered, but woe betide anyone foolish or brave enough to park alongside what is quite a small ground.

The driver marched off to the pavilion, where I dare say his issue was addressed with both courtesy and concern, as he emerged a few minutes later and made his way back to his car, possessed of a relatively calm and relaxed demeanour.

The New Ifield innings continued without any further serious incident, before we adjourned for tea mid afternoon.

The English cricket tea is a source of great pride amongst villages and clubs all over the country and rarely is any trouble or expense spared in its preparation or presentation. This day Meopham put on a spread that included sandwiches, cakes, muffins, crisps, soft drinks, tea and coffee. I reckon I have attended weddings in Australia that weren't as generously catered. I just wish they had bigger plates, as that might have saved me the trouble of piling on a third helping.

The designated thirty minutes flew by and we soon took the field again. Me with a poppy seed muffin stuffed in my trouser pocket.

The second innings passed without any great drama and the match concluded with everyone shaking hands before we retired to the bar in the pavilion.

It was well and truly dark by the time I left, having enjoyed a good few pints of the local beer and I was only too happy to accept a lift home, before returning the next day to collect the van.

It was terrific getting to know some of the players and club officials and the MCC connection made it a really special occasion.

Village greens and cricket grounds lie at the very heart of towns and hamlets all over the country and for me it was both a delight and a privilege to umpire a cricket match in England. I felt I had a made a small contribution in the very birth place of a game with such a wonderful history and a rich tradition.

It's a good thing that tree fell over.

CHAPTER 20

OVERLOADED

It didn't come as a great surprise when Jason's family bailed out of the UK and flew home. They had only stuck at the whole overseas adventure for a few months but had clearly been very unhappy from the outset.

An unwelcome distraction at the best of times, it was a shame that it should coincide with the launch of our first few franchises.

Jason would stay on for the time being and fly home in a month or so. Thereafter, he planned to commute back and forth between Australia and the UK, staying in each country for about six weeks at a time. I didn't think for a moment it could possibly work, to say nothing of the fact we would be incurring significant travel costs and the house our company was renting in Eynsford would sit vacant for much of the time.

There was little if anything I could do. I was a minority shareholder in a fledgling business and still finding my way when it came to marketing and managing a national franchise network. I wasn't drawing a salary from the company and I had an expensive flat in Sevenoaks to maintain, so I simply had to keep mowing and gardening during the day and come into the office at evenings and weekends, particularly when Jason was away.

Happily we had a company based in York taking the bulk of our phone calls for job leads and franchise enquiries, while Jason and I put together information packs to send out to those who had expressed an interest.

We had no shortage of prospects on the books, but of course it costs nothing to enquire and it was frustrating to work through a list of names, only to find that ours was often one of about thirty such information packs that some people had requested. It took no small amount of time, sorting those with genuine potential from the time wasters and it was very tempting to ask for the information to be returned when it clearly had no chance of being acted upon.

The handful of franchisees that were already operating had made solid starts and over time I came to realise that the recruitment process was very much a numbers game. Of every hundred people that enquired, we would probably meet face to face with no more than five and could expect to sign one. Numbers four and five we effectively discouraged, though most of those people had come to the conclusion that Jim's Mowing wasn't the right opportunity for them in any case. It was numbers two and three that used to break my heart. They were invariably bright, intelligent and capable people, possessed of all the qualities we were looking for, but more often than not they simply didn't have the courage to make the leap from secure full time employment.

I couldn't help but think if we were presenting a similar opportunity to people in Australia, we would be beating them off with a stick but I suppose that being from Melbourne and having seen the enormous success Jim's Mowing had become (more or less first hand), that perhaps my rather grand UK ambitions were a little unrealistic.

I was too busy working to be driving Jason to and from Heathrow and when he next flew back to Australia I was meeting with Philip Walker and his wife in Sevenoaks.

Mr Walker had worked with one of the major banks for several years and accepted an early retirement package that enabled him and his wife to spend much of their time in France. He was a keen gardener and wanted me to look after their lawns while they were away.

The Walkers had decided to embark on a rather grand plan of their own. Their front garden was planted on quite a steep slope and it was populated with huge dark green conifer trees that often cast a shadow over the house. The trees dominated the landscape and there was no room and no point in trying to grow anything underneath them. Their plan was to cut them all down, grind out the stumps and start afresh with an entirely new array of colourful plants and shrubs.

I was flattered the Walkers would even consider me to

do the job and I immediately referred the tree work to a local firm I had developed a relationship with. Down to Earth was based on a farm near Shoreham and they had all of the expertise, equipment and personnel to make short work of the task at hand. Once they had cleared the site, I would have a blank canvas to work with and given I had yet to gather any real knowledge of plants, I commissioned my friend Sarah from the local garden centre to help. She was a qualified horticulturist who had helped me out several times before with some useful advice and the odd crash course in gardening over the telephone.

I explained everything to the Walkers and they seemed perfectly happy with the arrangement. Down to Earth would clear the site and Sarah would design the garden, while I planted everything out and installed a watering system.

Sarah and I inspected the garden together on her day off. Once it was all cleared, the area looked twice the size but my friend clearly had everything under control. She had ascertained the acidity of the soil and considered the angle of the slope, measured against the shape and height that the plants she was suggesting would eventually grow to. Her plan would ensure the garden was never devoid of colour, as any shrubs that would be dormant in the colder months would be compensated by others that bloomed at that time of year.

She certainly sold the concept to me and the Walkers seemed equally impressed, asking us to go ahead. Sarah ordered all of the plants, while I would prepare the ground by digging in a great load of compost – and I knew just where to get it.

I had been dumping all of my green waste at the local tip for twenty pounds a load and this was my first opportunity to come full circle and buy some of it back. I left all of my equipment in the garage with the exception of a shovel, a rake and a wheelbarrow and drove into the trade section of the Sundridge Household Waste Facility.

Mountains of steaming compost were piled just inside the trade entrance and I went in search of the tip monster. He was sitting behind the wheel of his front end loader 'reading' a top shelf magazine. The compost was normally thirty pounds a tonne but apparently 'today' I could have two for the price of one.

I followed the monster back to the furthest pile and parked the truck as he instructed. He then scooped up a great pile of compost in his 'bucket' and tipped it in the back of my vehicle. I could see the body sink under its weight and thought for a moment that I might be better off taking it away as two separate loads but before I could act upon my instincts, he had dumped another load in the back and I was parting with my cash.

The monster gave me a receipt and I climbed into the cab as he left. Just sitting there I could feel a tremendous weight behind me. I started the engine, vowed to take it slowly and drove off. I reckon I had travelled about three feet before realising there was a problem. The truck could barely move and I had to rev the engine mercilessly just to gain the slightest bit of movement. With the motor fairly screaming beneath my feet, I managed to build up enough pace to actually register something on the dash. I had to. There was a speed hump just ahead. Given the circumstances it might just as well have been The Matterhorn. I thought I was no better than an even money chance to get over it and tried to convince myself that if I could, it would be all downhill from there. Just how the gentle slope of a small lump of concrete was supposed to propel me another five miles I really can't say but I did manage to get over the hump and out through the gate.

By this stage I had gathered a degree of momentum, although there was a terrible burning smell. I thought it must be the weight of the box rubbing against the rear tyres. Later I would discover that it was not in fact the tyres that were burning to a crisp but the clutch.

I negotiated no less than three more speed humps and made my way - albeit desperately slowly, out of the main entrance but the modest gradient of the road leading up to the A25 proved too much. I revved the engine as hard as I could and literally pushed against the steering wheel, but the burning sensation was now such that I felt sure something was about to explode, so I pulled into a lane that ran behind a row of houses, stopped the engine and got out.

The lane itself was covered with grass and it clearly didn't see much traffic, which was just as well, as I certainly wasn't going anywhere for the time being.

My only option was to offload the compost, or at least enough of it that I could actually drive the truck. The lane

I had pulled into was very narrow and there was no way I could possibly turn around. As it led to a dead end I would have to shovel most of the compost out of the back, over the top of the cab and onto the ground, otherwise I wouldn't be able to reverse out.

As it happens, the nursery where Sarah worked was about half a mile away and I was able to borrow a couple of hefty sacks that I might be able to sling the compost into. I didn't dare ask the tip monster for any help, as I couldn't imagine he would be allowed to take his loader off site and given where I had parked the truck he wouldn't have been able to access it anyway. To say nothing of the fact I was far too embarrassed.

I set the sacks out in front of the truck, climbed into the back and tossed the compost over the top of cab, one shovel load at a time. Most of it landed where I was aiming but by the same token, I think it is fair to say there is no better fed grassy lane in the country.

After about an hour, I had emptied two thirds of the load and felt brave enough to try again. I left two huge sacks full of compost sitting in the middle of the lane and reversed out. Happily the clutch held together and I gingerly made my way to the Walker's, who (as fate would have it) had a property with a particularly steep driveway. I stopped outside and allowed everything to cool - engine, clutch, tyres and me, before making the final ascent.

I made it to the top of the drive, opened the rear doors and went into shovel mode again, this time into a wheelbarrow which I pushed across the lawn and tipped over onto the recently cleared slope at the front of the house.

Once I had cleared the load, I crudely raked it over the garden bed and returned to the lane. Reversing in, I shovelled the contents of one of the bags into the back of the truck, drove to the Walker's and repeated the exercise – twice. With all the compost now finally in place, I raked it over and forked it all in, mixing it thoroughly with the soil.

All of the plants were delivered the following week and Sarah was kind enough to number each one corresponding to the diagram on her plan, which was wise, as names were rather wasted on me.

I stood all the plants in the back of the truck, drove to the Walker's and placed each one in position. It was nice to see the garden starting to take shape and given most of the plants were already quite large, it wasn't difficult to see how everything might look in another year or two.

Once I had planted each one, I turned my attention to installing a watering system, which was about fifty metres of black plastic tube, fitted with various drip points and junction brackets.

The idea was to connect a garden hose to the tubing, which would then snake around the base of each plant. Each tube would be pierced and fitted with numerous drip points and plugged at its end, so that the water was dispersed evenly throughout the whole garden.

I cut the tube into three lengths, plugged each end and connected them to a T shaped bracket. I then lay the tubes across the bed, twisting each one around the base of the plants until such time as I was satisfied that they were all accommodated.

It was a difficult exercise but eventually, everything was in place. I connected the hose, switched on the tap and stood back. Before long the water started to drip and run down the slope and I ran along the length of each tube just to make sure there was sufficient pressure to ensure all of the plants would get a decent soaking.

I was surprised to see water dripping quite freely from some sections but not from others. I climbed up and assuming that water pressure was the problem, turned the tap on full. The effect of which was that water freely streamed from the same sections as before but not at all from the others. By now, most of the soil was so wet that it was impractical to try and climb down the slope to inspect the system, so I explained to the Walkers that I would need to address a small water pressure problem the following day when the soil had dried out.

I went home and sketched a crude plan of the system. The water was reaching the top of slope okay and there were no kinks in the hose at all. The whole layout was aided by gravity, yet some sections that effectively ran up hill were working while some of the lower portions were not. I simply couldn't understand it.

I didn't solve the mystery until the following day when I walked around the garden, lifting each length of tube and tracing it back to the original bracket the hose was connected to. At first I thought the problem must be the bracket itself but eventually I realised that what I had in fact done was connect both ends of the same tube to the one bracket, which in short meant that it was feeding back onto itself and that I had an entire length, littered with numerous drip points, that in actual fact wasn't connected to anything.

I made the necessary adjustments, switched on the tap and then proudly informed Mr and Mrs Walker that I had managed to overcome the water pressure problem.

CHAPTER 21

TONBRIDGE FESTIVAL

My next umpiring appointment was in fact one of a series of games to be played at Tonbridge School, one of the most expensive and privileged educational institutions in the country.

Each year's 'Cricket Festival' saw Tonbridge play host to teams representing schools from Australia, South Africa and England.

This year the roster included St. Peter's Adelaide, Chester House from Cape Town and the Millfield School from Somerset.

Each school would play the other once on each of three consecutive days, with two games staged simultaneously. One played on the school's main ground - 'The Head' and another on an adjoining ground known as 'Martins.'

It was hard to imagine a more perfect setting for a game and I was thrilled to be appointed to 'The Head' on the first day.

Tonbridge played host to Chester House and I was rostered to stand with Joe Townsend, the 'Homework Tsar' from the training course and an umpire with some thirty years of experience, which included any number of county second eleven championship matches. No pressure then.

'The Head' was located at the very heart of the school grounds and opposite a limestone chapel that in any other setting could probably pass for a cathedral.

An impressive scoreboard was housed on the first level of the pavilion, above the dressing rooms, while an assortment of cars, parents and spectators were dotted around the boundary.

The pitch itself was immaculate and the outfield lush and green, as soon after the toss, the two teams followed Joe and me onto the field.

I took up a position at the northern end, securing the honour of the day's first over and was busily taking in the surrounds when I heard a voice call out in the distance.

'Sir.'

I thought one of the boys was addressing a teacher, as nothing resonated with me.

'Sir!' the voice repeated, a little louder this time, as my eyes scanned the chapel and its neighbouring buildings.

'Excuse me. Umpire!' the bowler shouted.

I turned around sharply.

'Oh. I'm sorry' I said. 'Are you talking to me?'

Needless to say, I granted his request for a practice run through. After all, manners should count for something.

The first innings saw Tonbridge accumulate a healthy score of 234 from 45 overs, before we adjourned to the pavilion for a roast lunch. It was the boy's responsibility to serve their teachers and the umpires and I made a point of consuming just the one glass of wine, lest there be any suggestion of influence during the afternoon session.

Forty minutes later we returned for the second innings, whereupon some of the Tonbridge boys seemed to enjoy the nick names I had invented for them and written on my bowling card. 'Curly' and 'Lefty' certainly did. As for 'Smart Arse' I am not so sure.

I was lucky enough to be appointed to 'The Head' for the second day and on the third I was allocated to the game on 'Martins.'

The match may have been scheduled on the school's second ground but if I ever umpire a game as exciting and enjoyable again, I will count myself very lucky.

Chester House from Cape Town was sent in by St. Peter's Adelaide, making 227 runs before we enjoyed another sumptuous lunch.

St. Peters' made steady progress in the run chase but lost wickets at regular intervals, which kept the result very much in the balance throughout.

Word had got around that a close finish was likely to ensue and after the match on 'The Head' finished early, a large crowd of players, parents and students surrounded 'Martins.'

The match came down to the last over. St. Peters needed 10 runs to win but with nine wickets down, just one mistake would end the day for the South Australians.

I was standing at the striker's end when the Chester House captain entrusted the crucial last over to his talented leg spinner, a fellow who had claimed a number of scalps earlier in the day.

The St. Peter's batsman took a brave and aggressive approach, trying to hit the first ball of the over into a neighbouring post code.

He missed and the ball landed safely in the wicket keeper's gloves.

The next delivery was called and signalled 'wide,' before the following was clipped through the leg side for two.

Four balls remaining. Seven runs to win.

Another 'wide' served only to increase the tension, before the next delivery yielded a single.

Three balls left and five runs to win.

Another ambitious swing and another miss followed before a repeat dose on the next delivery secured a thick edge past the keeper, over the slips and across the boundary for four.

The scores were tied with one delivery remaining.

I can remember thinking what a fabulous three days it had been, what a tremendous game I was witnessing and that conversations on the long flights home for both teams the next day, would surely be liberally punctuated with the outcome of this game in particular.

St. Peter's needed just a single to win and I was surprised to see the striker dance down the pitch just as the bowler tossed the ball in the air. One run would win the day. Hitting a six was just showing off.

The striker planted his left foot in the middle of the pitch and hurled his bat at the ball, completing a wide arc as his arms came full circle, all but throwing himself off balance in the process. Suffice to say he missed and stranded a good three metres out of his crease, could only watch as the ball travelled towards the stumps.

As it happened, the wicket keeper (in his haste to take hold of the ball and stump the striker), managed to dislodge the bails a split second before the ball itself hit the stumps.

Strictly speaking that is a 'No Ball' and I (as the striker's end umpire) was obliged under the laws of the game, to call and signal just that, effectively awarding a one run penalty to the batting side. The ball itself would be considered 'dead' upon the call, the batsman rendered 'not out' and as a consequence St. Peter's would win the day.

I did no such thing.

I clearly saw the keeper knock the bails off, as the striker himself was stranded way out of his ground. The ball ultimately hit the stumps and but for the keeper's indiscretion the batsman would have most certainly been bowled.

I had no desire to ruin what was (to my mind) a very fair and memorable outcome to a great game and I simply pretended that I didn't see what happened.

Happily no one else seemed to notice. All the players

shook hands and the overall mood amongst them and several hundred spectators was warm and friendly.

At least it was until the Chester House coach came onto the field. He marched towards the umpires and began berating my colleague for calling two wides in the last over when (apparently) he hadn't 'called one all day!'

His manner was very aggressive and he seemed almost out of control when I stepped in to defend my colleague.

'Now hang on a minute mate' I said, as I prepared to confess the crime that would have otherwise gifted the Adelaide boys a win.

He turned towards me and faced me with a wild, startled glare. It looked to me as if his eyes were likely to fall out of their sockets any moment.

'You' he said excitedly, pointing his finger in my face. 'You!'

I pinned my shoulders back, as I summoned an appropriate response should he say anything more.

'You' he continued 'are the best umpire we've had on our whole trip!'

He took hold of my hand, shook it furiously, said 'Thank you' and walked away.

That evening I gave John Allen a call.

During the training course, John and his colleagues had often referred to 'Law 43' - an apocryphal law of common sense that cricket umpires should seek to apply wherever possible in delicate and difficult situations.

I proudly told John that I had in fact that very day invented 'Law 44.'

'Law 44?' he asked. 'What on earth is that?

'Law 44' I repeated. 'If he sees fit, the umpire can do what he bloody well likes.'

CHAPTER 22

PAVING THE WAY

I had by now become great friends with a number of my clients. None more so than Stephanie Beattie who was gradually giving her property a thorough outdoor makeover.

Stephanie was kind, generous and grateful for anything I was able to do for her.

She progressed with each individual aspect of the exercise, as and when her finances allowed. To date she had erected a new fence, a pergola, turfed the back lawn and replanted the garden beds, when she asked if I could help her by laying a section of paving at the bottom of her garden. Paving wasn't exactly my long suit but I had seen and heard about some of the excellent hard landscaping jobs that Jody Chrich had completed and asked him to help.

Jody was developing his own franchise and building a base of clients in Swindon but it was still early days and I was able to encourage him across to Sevenoaks with the promise of a daily fee, a couple of take away meals and the opportunity to sleep on my sofa bed.

In the meantime, Stephanie and I paid a visit to Richard Abel's yard, where she selected a range of Indian Sandstone and a couple of Oak beams that would define the border of the lawn. We arranged for delivery to coincide with Jody's arrival and I freed up a couple of days in the diary.

Jody stayed overnight at my flat and we arrived on site the next day. Before long before all of the materials were delivered and we had equipped ourselves with all that we were likely to need.

Stephanie's property backed onto a narrow lane that was quite difficult to access, so we had forty odd sandstone slabs and a large bag of hard core scalpings lifted from Richard Abel's lorry and left around the corner.

The sandstone was housed in makeshift timber crates, which we had to break apart before we could cart each slab into position, while the only way to transport the shingle was a wheelbarrow load at a time.

Jody set about clearing and levelling the ground, while I carried each slab, leaning them against the fence.

Once we had the site smooth and level, we barrowed in all the hard core, raked it over and pummelled it into the ground with what the hire shop called a 'whacker plate,' - a flat bed of stainless steel, connected to a petrol motor and set of handle bars. Once we started it up the steel plate vibrated like mad, bouncing up and down as it squashed all the shingle and soil flat and level. It was an exercise that otherwise might have taken us the best part of a day and one that was completed in less than ten minutes. I might have joked the 'whacker plate' looked like some kind of giant massage implement but it certainly did the trick.

Jody started sorting through the slabs leaving me to blend the mix of cement and ballast in the wheelbarrow.

It was quite exciting to see him set the first slab in place, as I had never even conceived of undertaking a job like this before. He smeared each slab's base with mortar and pressed it firmly against the hard core base, using a spirit level to confirm its integrity. A second slab was laid, then a third and a forth. Before long we had created one complete edge and were working our way across to the other side. The project was certainly taking shape and it looked tremendous. By the time we had used up two barrow loads of mortar, about three quarters of the job had been completed but it was getting dark and Jody was anxious to get back home, so he left me to finish everything off the next day.

After a quick refresher course in cement ratios, we tidied everything up and went our separate ways.

I returned the next day and confirmed that each slab we had laid was level and set firmly in place. I then mixed the cement and ballast in the barrow just as I had the previous day, I smeared the same amount on the base of each slab and on the scalpings, just as we had the previous day and followed the same procedure in confirming that each one was level. So why didn't it work?

It all looked fine to me, so I left it all to set and meticulously cleaned and cleared everything away.

The next morning Stephanie rang to say that she thought the paving and beams looked fabulous but that some of the slabs were loose and wobbly. No prizes for guessing which ones.

My site visit confirmed that all the slabs Jody had laid were set like stone, while all of mine were not. I could stand perfectly still on all of his and make the finals of a dance contest on most of mine.

I lifted each loose slab to find the mortar had stuck to the base and for the most part it was set against the hard core okay but for some reason it just wasn't holding together. All I could think was that I had got the mix wrong, possibly adding too much (or too little) water. In any case I lifted each one and started again.

I mixed the mortar in the barrow, smeared the bases again and battled to make each one level. Once again it all looked fine when I had finished and once again (when I checked the next day) they were all loose, wobbly and easily lifted.

Clearly cement and I just didn't get on and the last thing I wanted was for Stephanie to suffer a fall, so I rang Jody and asked him to (once again) drive across from Swindon and fix it all for me.

It was proving to be a good investment that sofa bed.

Jason was soon in Australia again and I was working my way through our franchise enquiries as best I could. Already our modest network ranged in age from mid twenties to mid fifties and there was certainly no 'typical' franchisee, as we were clearly attracting people from a diverse range of backgrounds.

Training was proving to be an issue however. Some of our franchisees brought a useful array of skills and experience with them but the important aspect for us was that they had a solid and clear understanding of just how the whole Jim's system was structured and how it all worked. Our preference had been for anyone planning to join us to travel to Australia beforehand but that simply wasn't practical for many of them, even if we did effectively cover the cost.

All the same, by this stage two of our very first franchisees had taken the opportunity to secure regional franchise rights. One took on a sector that comprised much of East Sussex and Surrey, while the other secured the rights to most of Norfolk and Suffolk.

It was encouraging that two people had sufficient faith in the brand and the business to make such a substantial investment after only operating for about six months but by the same token we were still very much hamstrung by Jason's situation. He was spending as much time in Australia as he was in the UK, which was proving to be very expensive and I was finding it difficult to keep everything on track while finding the time to operate my own franchise and simply pay the rent.

CHAPTER 23

THE UMPIRING CAPER

John Allen and I had kept in regular contact, as he continued to present me with any number of weekend umpiring opportunities for the months ahead.

I gratefully accepted each one and discovered (once I had typed up the list and stuck it on the fridge) that I had in fact committed to umpiring every Saturday and Sunday for the remainder of the season.

My appointments were to various village, social and school fixtures at clubs and grounds located in Kent and Sussex. Saturday games were competitive matches, while Sundays were generally reserved for friendlies.

The context of the games made little difference to me, as I was simply delighted to be there at all, while I managed to discover any number of hidden gems within the towns and villages of England's south east.

I became an occasional fixture with a touring team known as 'The Chessmen' who were for the most part in the twilight of their playing careers.

They toured around the county playing Sunday friendlies and we became well acquainted, as a consequence of the obligatory post match pint, as much as anything that transpired on the field.

Chessmen matches were invariably played in a scrupulously fair manner. My umpiring role was often reduced to simply counting the balls in the over, as batsmen would invariably walk when caught behind or trapped plumb LBW.

I can remember one Chess Batsman playing at ball that a moment later landed safely in the wicket keeper's gloves. Without so much as a murmur from the bowler or fielding side, he tucked his bat under his arm and marched off the field. I thought he must have a train to catch but it later transpired that the ball had in fact just barely brushed his glove.

Each game I umpired seemed to be played in a setting that was even more quaint and picturesque than the last.

Cricket grounds were often bordered by trees that were centuries old and in one instance a gentle stream ran along the length of the boundary.

Shipbourne Cricket Club leased the superbly named 'Fatting Pen Field' from the Fairlawne Estate - a fair patch of dirt, once owned by a family of National Hunt racehorse trainers that numbered the Queen Mother among their clients.

The club was sponsored by a pub in the village, appropriately called 'The Chaser' where players, opponents and umpires would invariably convene after each game.

Shipbourne became a regular fixture (both home and away) and I soon became great friends with the club's players and officials.

Many were old boys of Tonbridge School, commuting from London each weekend to play.

'Fatting Pen Field' itself, was set back about a mile from the road, beyond an obscure entrance that many a visiting team took a while to locate. Games often failed to start on time, after any number of players arrived late. An anomaly that wasn't helped by the fact the locals would often refuse any knowledge of just where the club was located, if those asking failed to pronounce the name of the village correctly.

In addition to my weekend endeavours, I often stood in a Friday night fixture with the 'Old Oaks.' All of whom were ageing and former players of Sevenoaks Vine.

The Sevenoaks cricket ground was a five minute walk from my flat, my match fee was free beer and I had the opportunity to stand with Ian Fraser, who first introduced me to the training course some months before.

'Old Oaks' games were played at a fairly gentle pace and on one occasion they inducted a young Australian into their ranks, before he joined the senior team on Saturdays.

He was a nineteen year old leg spinner/batsman from New South Wales, who had been living and playing 'up north' before relocating to the south east for the remainder of the season.

Quiet and softly spoken, he came on to bowl at my

end and I remember how I could hear the ball literally fizz out of his hand, such were the revolutions he managed to impart on it.

When he came in to bat, he confidently advanced down the wicket to the very first ball he faced, clipping it through mid wicket with precise timing.

I emailed a friend who lived in London the next day, suggesting he remember this kid's name, as I felt sure he was destined to play for Australia.

His name was Steven Smith.

The following day, I returned to the village ranks when I was appointed to stand in a game at Shoreham, a small village just north of Sevenoaks. Happily not too far north, as I chose to walk home after consuming several pints of the 'Dartford Wobbler' – a guest beer from a local micro brewery that was on tap at the King's Head, where we gathered from late afternoon when the game was washed out.

The pub itself was built in 1570 and I wasn't able stand upright in the bar, such was the height of the ceiling. I remained perched on a stool until the pub closed and it was time to stagger home.

Rain had interrupted play a couple of times earlier in the day, whereupon we decided to take an early tea.

I didn't particularly take to the spread of multi grain, cucumber, cheese and pickle sandwiches and instead began piling a number of white bread and jam concoctions on my plate, when I felt a tap on my shoulder.

'Excuse me' a very gentle and kind looking woman said, 'but those are actually for the children.'

I looked down at the forlorn and disappointed face that belonged to a girl who looked about six. She was holding a small empty plate in front of her chest, as were another four or five of her contemporaries who had very politely queued behind her. It must have looked like a scene from Oliver Twist.

I have rarely felt so ashamed.

My association with Ian Fraser and the Old Oaks was to pay a healthy dividend later that season however, when I was invited to umpire a couple of mid week matches on the Vine.

The Sevenoaks Cricket Club had arranged to stage a charitable event with 'Lashings,' a touring group of former international cricketers who played against various club teams as a means of generating funds for charity.

Ian and I would umpire free of charge, while the club would sell tickets to the matches and tables for lunch where guests would be seated with players and entertained by Zimbabwean international Henry Olanga's singing.

The Lashings player roster included the likes of Gordon Greenidge, Devon Malcolm and Phil De Freitas, with Australia represented by Stuart Law and Ian Harvey.

The weather was kind and the event drew a large crowd that gathered around the boundary for matches either side of lunch, against members of the Sevenoaks first and second elevens.

It was quite a thrill to umpire a game with players whose autographs I had sought as child, even if their pace and veracity had dulled somewhat.

CHAPTER 24

RESTRUCTURING

We battled on for several months and to Jason's credit he certainly did all he could to find someone who might be interested in securing his share of the business. His position was made all the more difficult by the fact he had effectively 'sold' the opportunity to a number of minority shareholders in Australia and I can't imagine any of them would have been all that thrilled to know what was happening.

Jim's Mowing was still very much in its infancy and given it was located and operating in the UK, not a particularly attractive option for an Australian based investor. Similarly there really only a handful of people in the country who knew just how successful the Jim's model was elsewhere in the world.

The business was suffering and growth had stalled. Jason was flying back and forth to Australia every six weeks or so and he was clearly distracted while he was in the UK.

Over time however one of our regional franchisors expressed an interest and I did my best to broker a deal between them.

He wasn't prepared to buy Jason out altogether, so the three of us settled on a deal whereby he would secure an initial stake from Jason and thereafter retain the option to purchase the balance of his shares from future earnings. It meant that he now held a controlling interest and that eventually he and I would own the entire business.

It was a reasonable outcome and everyone seemed happy with the arrangement. We signed the relevant documents and Jason flew back to Australia.

Logistically it would prove awkward as my new business partner was based hundreds of miles away in Norfolk, but at the time it was the best we could do and the only option we had.

I had by now started to scale back the operation of my own franchise as I was spending a lot more time in the office before we employed a full time administrator.

Cathy Smith was one of several candidates that a local recruitment company had put forward. She lived nearby, was very experienced, capable and over time developed an excellent relationship with all of our franchisees.

One of her first tasks was to organise an event where we could present the new ownership structure to our existing network, together with our plans and goals for the future.

We settled on a Paintball venue in Buckinghamshire, as

it was geographically equidistant for most of us and featured an area where we could convene for lunch and make a short presentation before we set about shooting one another.

The day was a great success and the first part of our plan to sure up some important relationships. The second element that we were anxious to complete was for Jim himself to be happy and comfortable with the fact that a new team had effectively taken over the UK operation.

As luck would have it, Jim's Group was staging an Australian national conference in a few weeks time and we decided that I should attend.

I caught a plane to Melbourne and soon after flew to the Gold Coast. I checked into the venue and wandered downstairs just as the four day event was due to start. I stopped by the registration desk and said hello to Greg Puzzolo, who said he was delighted to see me as Jim was ill, he had returned to Melbourne and that I would be replacing him on stage to open the event.

I spotted Jason soon after, who confirmed that in a last minute change to the schedule he and I would be hoisted on stage in front of some five hundred delegates and armed with a microphone. Given he was holding several pages of carefully written notes at the time, I think it was fair to assume he had been given a little more notice than me.

Even so, I quite enjoyed the experience. Jason and I sat together on a couch while Greg stood behind a lectern 'interviewing' us both. It was quite good fun and given the fact I had just flown in from the other side of the world, I did rather enjoy my new found celebrity.

I took part in all of the social activities and workshops, meeting people from various divisions and from all over Australia and New Zealand. The first night there we were treated to a cruise on the river, while on the second we attended a dinner in the hotel that was hosted by local impresario 'Dickie Dazzler,' complete with bad wig and a shiny silver suit. The event had a music theme, a trivia quiz and God forbid - a dancing competition.

Everyone seated on the six tables at the front of the room was given a number. I was number five. Over time, numbers one and three were asked to show off their dancing prowess, while the twos and fours were called upon for Karaoke. It was clear where my fate lay.

The number ones had to dance to Tina Turner's 'Nut Bush City Limits' and I was so terrified at the prospect of 'dancing' myself, that I can't even recall what the number threes were burdened with.

My eyes roamed the perimeter of the room. I was scanning the exits, as I desperately searched for an excuse not to take part. Needless to say I can't dance to save my life and am desperately self conscious in the general vicinity of a dance floor at the best of times. Let's just say the prospect of 'strutting my stuff' in front of five hundred Jim's Group delegates and partners, was about as appealing to me as cage fighting.

The second round of the Karaoke was truly awful and sure enough, the number fives would dance. Oh joy. I walked onto the floor, encouraged by my table colleagues, sweating so much I felt sure my feet would slip out of my shoes. Six of us lined up in front of the stage, as I stared at the floor. None of us knew what the music track would be and I vowed that if the 'Birdie Dance' struck up I would be on my way to the airport before the votes were in.

Thank God for The Village People. I mean even I can dance to YMCA. All I had to do was march up and down on the spot until the chorus kicked in and then give it up large with the alphabet bit. As those first few bars thumped out of the speakers, I can't recall ever feeling so relieved. I marched with passion and purpose, defining each letter as if there was no tomorrow. As far as I was concerned, mine was a standout performance and it was all I could do not to demand a recount when I wasn't presented with the trophy.

CHAPTER 25

FOOT IN MOUTH

I returned to the UK and set about trying to achieve a balance between mowing and office work. I needed the gardening work to pay the rent but by the same token the more time and effort I could invest in recruiting franchisees the more likely it was the business would succeed.

I managed to retain most of my regular clients and now afforded myself the luxury of only doing one off jobs for people that I liked (or at the very least found attractive) and who were prepared to pay whatever I quoted.

No disrespect to Mrs Annett but she didn't exactly tick all of those boxes.

She was a nice old lady (half blind and largely deaf) who lived in Shoreham. Her niece worked in the accounts department at Godfrey's and she had been let down and ripped off by any number of contractors before. I agreed to help her out as a favour, even though she contradicted pretty much every qualifying criterion I had recently set. With the sole exception of the fact she was single.

Her property was an absolute jungle. The grass was more than a foot long, the garden beds were hopelessly overgrown and there were several hidden threats lurking throughout, in the shape of rusted sheets of iron, rocks, stones and an abandoned shopping trolley. The job didn't call for garden maintenance so much as guerrilla warfare.

Mrs Annett wanted the garden beds tidied up and all the grass to be neatly mown. It was a task that had clearly seen off a few predecessors and one I simply didn't have the time to do. Even so, I didn't want to let her down and I proposed to come by each week and do what I could, until such time as the 'lawns' could sustain a fortnightly service, a time frame that by any realistic measure could be quantified in years.

She seemed grateful that I was prepared to make any sort of commitment and kept me supplied with generous quantities of tea and cordial throughout my tenure.

Mrs Annett was one client who had her own catch phrase. She owned a small dog. It was yappy, small, fluffy and white and it barked and growled at every opportunity. It was impossible to say hello, accept a drink or simply chat without her taking time out to berate the little beast. Every exchange we ever had (no matter how brief), was invariably punctuated with cries of 'Shuddup Ginny!' Needless to say each one made not the slightest difference.

Another client that managed to 'slip under the radar' of my new regime, was Gus and Linda Thorogood.

They lived in a small cottage in Stone Street that adjoined a large orchard. Mrs Thorogood worked with a customs and shipping agent in London, while her husband was retired, having spent several years working at Australia House in The Strand. These days Gus got around in a Volvo Estate but in the past he had driven a succession of diplomats to and from various appointments in something a bit grander.

The Thorogoods bred 'Clumber Spaniels' for show and they had one quite successful graduate in residence at the time. As far as I can tell, the 'Clumber' is a relatively obscure breed and I reckon quite an intelligent and perceptive one, as the whole time I worked there it was clear their prized show dog would never forgive me for calling him 'Bucket Head.' He had returned from a trip to the vet one day with a plastic cone strapped around his neck (hence the derogatory remark) and I swear he took great offence to it. To that point we had got along perfectly well but thereafter he growled and threatened me at every opportunity. Very sensitive breed the Clumber.

Gus and I became great mates and I took his incredible rudeness to be an indication of genuine affection. He derided and rubbished the quality of my work at every opportunity, rolled his eyes at the prospect of making me a cup of tea and relished telling me that I 'couldn't run a bath let alone a business.'

In between insults he showed me his workshop where he hand crafted all manner of implements in wood and invited me inside the house to show me his various war time naval memorabilia. We spent as much time talking to one another as I ever did working and I was often presented with a cup of tea as soon as I arrived, whereupon Gus and I would sit together in the garden. More than once I had thanked him for the tea, handed him my empty cup and started to leave before realising that I hadn't yet in fact done any work.

I had by now managed to free up a couple of days each week to spend in the office and to travel around the country. In the office, I enjoyed speaking with new customers on the phone and allocating job leads to franchisees on our computer system. It gave me a sense that the advertising we were co-ordinating was working and it was very satisfying to see our franchisees deriving a benefit from all that we were doing.

The diversity of accents I encountered could be challenging enough, but I was well and truly stumped one afternoon when a customer rang the office having seen one of our ads in a local village magazine. A gentleman wanted someone to come out and give him a quote to 'trim the hedge and mow the lawn.'

'Certainly Sir' I responded, my fingers poised over the keyboard ready to enter his address details onto the system. 'We can help you with that' I said. 'Tell me, whereabouts are you located?'

'I'm at home' he said.

The job was eventually allocated to Keith Davies. Keith was an engineer from Liverpool who drove down with his wife to meet with us at the office a couple of months before.

Meetings with prospective franchisees generally took about an hour or two. Keith's took four. To describe his preparation as thorough would be a massive understatement. He had studied our information literature and arrived with one hundred and forty questions typed on four pages of A4 paper. Many were answered during the course of general conversation and any that were not we worked through on an individual basis. I considered it a great compliment (to the Jim's system), that after such a thorough investigation Keith decided to go ahead and invest in a franchise and it came as no surprise when he continued to make a tremendous success of it.

Soon after, I had a call from Trevor Middleton who gave a glowing report about a prospective franchisee that he had been showing the ropes to for the past couple of days.

Jon Dodd had asked us to send him some information about the franchise opportunity some months before but it wasn't until he saw Trevor's vehicle parked outside the garden centre that he presently managed, that he did anything about it.

Normally we would arrange induction days like his from the office, brokering a suitable date between a prospect and an experienced (wherever possible nearby) franchisee, but I had absolutely no recollection of Jon whatsoever and didn't have the first idea just who on earth Trevor was talking about.

I was far too embarrassed to admit as much over the

phone, as I had clearly forgotten the whole thing, but it soon transpired that he and Trevor had made all of the necessary arrangements themselves, which was perfectly fine with me, even if I did feel a bit surplus to requirements.

We were anxious by this stage to try and gather all of our franchisees and a number of our more genuine prospects together in order to build a kind of team ethic amongst us all. We had people operating from Sussex to Scotland and we were anxious to try and overcome the distances between us and draw everyone closer together.

I managed to broker a deal with my friends from Shipbourne Cricket Club and secure the use of their ground, pitch, equipment and pavilion for the inaugural 'Jim's Big Day Out.' The idea was to invite family members and divide our franchisees into two teams, before staging a cricket match with an engraved trophy awarded to the winning captain. We booked a jumping castle and a barbecue, together with tables, chairs, ice, beer, wine, soft drinks and salads.

What we needed was a roof.

In the finest traditions of the 'British Summer' it rained, on and off all day. We spent much of the time huddled together in the pavilion, while I made the occasional dash to the 'Beer Tent,' arguably providing the day's highlight, as I executed a spectacular back flip, landing in a puddle adjacent to the barbecue.

Another initiative we developed was a horticultural training course that each and every new franchisee would have the opportunity to attend. Many of our recruits had brought little or no gardening knowledge with them and we devised a three day course in conjunction with Hadlow College that was designed to give them a thorough (if relatively basic) induction and hopefully to provide a platform for further training.

We were very lucky that the course was designed and presented by Stephen Harmer, one of the college's most experienced and likeable lecturers. What Stephen didn't know about landscaping and gardening wasn't worth knowing but above all his presentation, style and overall demeanour provided an ideal fit.

Given we had people travelling from all over the country we agreed to put everyone up for two nights at a nearby hotel, which gave us all the opportunity to convene over dinner at one of the local pubs.

Everyone seemed to enjoy the event and it gave some of our guys the opportunity to ask questions of Stephen in a more relaxed and social environment. I was also able to let everyone know just who else we hoped to get on board and from which part of the country.

There was however a 'foot in mouth moment,' when I was bemoaning the fact that I sometimes had trouble deciphering some of the accents that populated the British Isles. At the time we were liaising with one particular prospect in Aberdeen, whom I couldn't even be sure was speaking English. Regrettably, I confessed over dinner, that having answered his call one day, I handed the phone to Cathy, insisting the person on the end of the line 'clearly suffers from some kind of learning disability.'

It was supposed to be a joke. Mind you judging by the look on the faces of the Scottish contingent, namely Alan Roberts from Glenrothes and Drew Glen, recently retired from the army and returned to Glasgow, it could have been a little more happily phrased.

CHAPTER 26

THE PLAYING CAPER

My first season of umpiring had been a tremendous success. I had enjoyed myself immensely, made any number of new friends and drunk quite a lot of beer.

My second season brought with it an opportunity to advance, when I was invited to umpire in the Kent League and also to play again.

Kent League games would be played on Saturdays, which left Sundays free to play village friendlies with Shipbourne.

It seemed like the perfect balance and save for the fact a few old muscles would have to come out hibernation, I fairly jumped at the chance.

Umpiring in the Kent League was a more professional endeavour, which meant attending meetings throughout the season and the prospect of sitting an oral exam.

I had breezed through my original multiple choice exam and arrived for my 'oral,' in a small room next to the kitchen in the Wateringbury church hall.

Two examiners sat behind a table, while I perched on a chair in front of them.

'Now you are in for a bit of a grilling' one of them said.

He wasn't kidding.

Three hours later, having visualised and explained countless match day scenarios, I found myself in the kitchen, nursing a thumping headache, as the examiners tallied my score.

Should I fail, I vowed never to return.

The tone was set early, as I was asked to explain what procedures and processes I should enact when first arriving at the ground and walking onto the field of play.

'What have you got with you?' one of the examiners asked.

I reeled off a list that included a counter, bowler's marker, a spare bail, pen and an overs card.

'You've forgotten something' he said.

I added 'a positive mental attitude and cheerful disposition' but he wasn't buying it.

'No. You've forgotten something' he said sternly.

'Beats me' I said

'The ball!' he replied.

I fired back 'My colleague's got it', pointing to an imaginary associate to my left.

I thought it was pretty funny.

They didn't.

I had of course already factored in a mandatory deduction for being an Australian but happily I managed to pass comfortably enough all the same.

The prospect of playing again wasn't quite as daunting and while I had already acquired a Shipbourne club shirt, sweater and cap, my shopping list was still quite long.

As luck would have it, the Bat and Ball sports shop was housed above the Godfreys show room in Sevenoaks and I had waved around any number of bats there in the past.

Most of the major brands were displayed, as was a name I wasn't the least bit familiar with.

Salix was a small Kent based outfit, owned and operated by a fellow called Andrew Kember, who apparently served an apprenticeship with legendary Sussex bat maker John Newbery.

I could pick up and recognise a Salix cricket bat blind folded. I am not entirely sure why but they just felt different. They seemed balanced and comfortable, as if they belonged in my hands and one Saturday morning I visited the factory.

I could have picked a better day and time. It was the eve of the cricket season and the showroom was awash with father's treating their sons and established clients either upgrading or dropping off bats to be repaired.

All the same, I was lucky enough to be introduced to Andrew, with whom I managed to strike an instant rapport.

I told him that picking up one of his bats was like being upgraded to Business Class and how much I admired the passion and craftsmanship that must be involved.

I explained that I was in the market for a bat myself, whereupon he escorted me into the factory and stood me in front of a shelved wall, full of crudely shaped 'clefts' of willow with bat handles already inserted.

He took each one out in turn, retaining a handful that he inspected more closely. Once he had narrowed the stock down to three or four he started hitting each with a wooden mallet, asking me to do the same and together we settled on one, where the mallet fairly bounced off the face of the blade.

Over the course of the next hour or so, he shaped, sanded and caressed a crude piece of willow into a bespoke masterpiece. He even filed and shaped the base of the handle to suit my own grip, asking me to feel the weight and balance at every stage.

His concentration was immense and he seemed to be in a hypnotic trance throughout, such was his focus and attention.

When the time came to pay, I added a bag, some pads and gloves, assured by one staff member that 'No one gets a bat made for them quite like that' and that mine was an indeed something special.

My new bat and I would debut in one of Shipbourne's Sunday friendlies, a week before the start of the Kent League season.

We were playing away at Speldhurst and having lost the toss, were asked to bowl first.

Our captain was kind enough to let me field in the slips. Not that I was ever likely catch anything but it did give me the opportunity to be closely involved in the game.

The match itself was very relaxed and friendly, while I noticed that a lot of the Speldhurst players were using bats that were branded 'Willo Stix,' with stickers of snakes and lizards plastered on the back of their blades.

When yet another batsman came to the crease with an Anaconda on his, I chirped 'Gee you must be getting a pretty deal on those bats.'

I expected to be ignored or at the very least treated to a stubborn, pithy reply but instead he stepped towards me, showed me the label on the face of his blade and said 'Yes, well they're made by a local company and we like to support them.'

Speldhurst put their 'Stix' to good use throughout the afternoon amassing 183 runs before it was time for tea.

I was slotted to bat at five and indulged in a few sandwiches and cakes, secure in the knowledge I wouldn't be required immediately after the break.

Our third wicket fell with the score on 73 and I strode to the crease to join Ben Spokes who was by this stage well set and half my age.

I managed to survive my first few deliveries, before deflecting a ball behind square leg and setting off for my first run.

I shuffled towards the pavilion end (where my team mates had gathered) and as Ben and I passed each other mid pitch, he glanced across and said 'Come on. Three.'

I hadn't reached the other end before I peered over my

shoulder and called back 'Three?!' What are you fucking kidding?!' as a burst of laughter erupted from the boundary.

Suffice to say we completed a comfortable two, which under the circumstances I found quite sufficient.

Once the running arrangements had been sorted out, we managed to compile a healthy partnership, before Ben departed with Shipbourne needing just two runs to win.

Andy Gillam came to the crease and simply refused to score. In fact at one point he stepped way across the pitch, allowing a ball that would otherwise have been called 'wide' to hit his leg.

At the end of the over, I asked what on earth he was doing. He explained that I was on 49 and that if he or sundries should score the winning runs, it would deny me the opportunity to make a 50 on debut.

I thought he was being very generous and told him so, when he confessed that his primary motivation was the fact I would be expected to buy at least two jugs of beer after the game if I did.

It would have been downright churlish to get out at that point and happily I managed to get us home in the next over.

The beer I was expected to buy was Harvey's Sussex Bitter. In fact, it was always Harvey's Sussex Bitter, given our fixture secretary only ever scheduled games with clubs who frequented pubs that had it on tap.

One of the nice aspects about umpiring in the Kent League was the opportunity to meet a number of first class and international players.

Niall O'Brien was one of them and we crossed paths when he was playing with Folkestone, shortly after keeping wicket for Ireland at the World Cup.

He was a talented player but an annoying commentator, as he felt obliged to keep us all constantly informed of his opinions and strategies from behind the stumps.

I was well tired of the constant chatter, to say nothing of his high pitched voice and piercing accent, when I managed to enact a small measure of revenge.

Knowing full well how precious wicket keepers can be when it comes to extras recorded against their name, I seized upon an opportunity when he was standing up to the stumps.

A bowler's delivery had clearly brushed the batsman's leg, before crossing the boundary for four runs, when I turned to the non striker and said 'Watch this.'

I turned around, faced the pavilion and signalled to the scorers with a raised open palm, secure in the knowledge they would record four 'byes' in the score book and pretty much ruin O'Brien's day.

It certainly had the desired effect, as he spent the next few minutes kicking at the turf and protesting the decision to anyone who would listen. I was branded a 'Feckin eejit' for my trouble but considered it a points victory all the same.

The following year I had a phone call in the office. It was from a very well spoken fellow whose name I didn't recognise and I slouched in my chair, fearing he was about to make a complaint against one of our franchisees.

'I'm from Kent County Cricket Club' he said, as I sharply sat bolt upright.

Apparently Kent had arranged to play two pre-season fixtures against Nottinghamshire and Northamptonshire and they needed an umpire.

No prizes for guessing the outcome of that conversation.

I arrived at the St. Lawrence ground in Canterbury to be greeted by Ken Amos, who was the head of the Kent League Umpires' Panel and three of my team mates from Shipbourne who took the day off work to watch.

Both teams comprised a handful of internationals and I was absolutely thrilled to be involved, particularly as I got to sign my very first (and to date only) autograph for a young boy who had secured a prime position outside the dressing rooms.

I returned a week later for the match against Northants and met Ken again in the Umpires' Room on the first level of the grandstand.

'There you go' he said, pointing at the back page of the local newspaper that he had hung on a coat hook.

I read the headline and the first few paragraphs of an article that clearly related to the Notts' game the week before.

'So? What of it?' I said.

'The photo' he replied.

I looked at a large colour photograph of Kent's

opening bowler Robbie Joseph, sending down a delivery the week before. Behind him stood the figure of a very tall umpire, wearing a white coat, a broad brimmed hat and an Australian MCC member's tie. His gaze was fixed with the most earnest concentration.

'Oh it's me!' I said excitedly.

CHAPTER 27

NO ACCOUNTING FOR TASTE

As much as I enjoyed servicing my mowing clients, to say nothing of the fact I needed the money, I had to step back from the practical side of things and focus on the business overall. We had taken over the operation of the UK admin centre which meant we were taking dozens of phone calls from clients and prospective franchisees and it was unfair to leave Cathy in the office on her own each day.

Andy Byrne had recently relocated to Surrey, when his father in law became ill and he was able to take over all of my regulars in and around Sevenoaks. It was a bit of a commute from Crawley but he would have a ready-made client base and a decent supply of tea and biscuits.

He never thanked me for handing him Mrs and Mrs Phillips as a client, but he did manage to update me with his various misadventures at 'Squirrels,' to say nothing of his ongoing campaign to get himself sacked.

To be fair, Andy probably suffered even more than me,

as he bore witness to various altercations with the neighbours and numerous spats between the two. I recall receiving a text message he sent me one hot day, having been confronted in the garden by a braless Young Mrs Phillips, wearing a skimpy cotton singlet and pair of pink Hot Pants that were hitched high above her waist. Andy described her outfit as like something out of 'Baywatch.' The mental picture I had was more akin to 'Nightmare on Elm Street.'

In the meantime, David Hughson was making great strides in Edinburgh and anxious to develop his business further he enrolled in a two day training course at Hadlow.

He accepted an invitation to stay a couple of nights in my flat and arrived with a plethora of Scottish goodies that he had picked up at the airport. It consisted of a bottle of Scotch, some delicious cheese, a packet of oat cakes and a Haggis.

I put the Scotch aside and devoured the cheese and biscuits in no time at all, while the Haggis stayed in the fridge for a bit. I was never too sure just when I should cook it. I knew something of its reputation and that many considered it 'an acquired taste.' I figured it was too risky to inflict on anyone else, so one Sunday evening I decided to treat myself.

All I really knew of Haggis was that whatever its contents, they were enshrined and subsequently cooked, in a sheep's stomach. So are you supposed to eat the stomach as well or just the contents? I had no idea what was inside, as all the label could offer was a flag of St. Andrew crowning the word Haggis, together with a sell by date that was (regrettably) some months in the future. For all I knew, there could be any number of different varieties, flavours and influences. Perhaps they ranged from hot and spicy to savoury and sweet. Is there a children's Haggis for example, one with chocolate chips or a dessert version that you serve with ice cream? It was all a mystery to me.

The one David had left me with was relatively small (about the same size as a large grapefruit) and quite heavy. 'Packed full of the Flavour and Spirit of the Highlands' I expect. In any case I peeled off the plastic wrapper and left it sitting in a saucepan full of boiling water, as per the instructions on the label.

Some twenty minutes later I was sitting at the table, knife and fork in hand, staring at the steaming beige blob that I had just plonked on a plate. It could not have looked any less appealing and I found it difficult to reconcile the fact that this was in fact 'dinner,' given it looked more like a tumour than a meal.

I poked at it with a fork and made an initial incision with my knife. The skin was actually quite thin and it severed easily enough, allowing a coarse, grey coloured mince to slowly ooze out. I cut it all the way across the top and from side to side, peeling the skin away to open the contents up completely. I was worried that it may not be cooked properly, so I picked through the mince with a fork, looking for any meat that was lighter or pink in colour. The bland, grey texture was entirely consistent throughout however, liberally dosed as it was with hundreds of tiny white pods that looked to me like insect larvae.

There was nothing I could see that I particularly wanted to put in my mouth (let alone swallow), but in the interests of curiosity and the fact that David might one day ask, I gathered a small portion on the end of my fork, threw caution to the wind and introduced it to my tongue.

It tasted like soil.

Completely devoid of any discernible flavour or texture, it was about as appealing as a spoonful of mud.

In the interests of fair play, I tried a second then a third portion. Each one smaller than the last and each one equally foul.

I had clearly reached an impassable cultural divide and could go no further, but satisfied that I could now claim to have 'eaten Haggis,' I promptly threw the rest of it in the bin, rang the Lantern Chinese Take Away and ordered the King Prawn with Cashew Nuts.

CHAPTER 28

BEATEN AND SHOT

We found ourselves particularly busy in the office throughout the spring and summer and took on a part time employee to help with all the phone calls and also to co-ordinate the local advertising activity for our growing number of franchisees.

Roma Twort brought her black Labrador in each day and often regaled us with stories of her weekend 'Pheasant Shoots.'

She travelled around the county working as 'a beater,' which meant she and her dog would stroll around the countryside trying to flush defenceless birds out of the scrub, so that some clown with a shotgun could blast them out of the sky. I thought it sounded like great fun and one day she arranged for me to come along.

We arrived at a property near Meopham that was owned by a fellow called Iva, a man who fitted the 'landed gentry' stereotype to a tee. He was an older gentleman, bearded with grey hair and a shotgun.

There were five or six 'Guns,' all dressed exactly the same (in buttoned tweed jackets with leather patches) and as many 'Beaters' (dressed more randomly), of which I was one.

Apparently the pheasants were born and reared in pens before being released to feed on the remnants of recently harvested crops and whatever they could scrounge in the forest, at least until the onset of 'the shooting season' anyway. Just how many might survive into next year would largely depend on how good a shot Iva and his chums were.

The 'Guns' took up designated positions at the bottom of a hill or the end of a field while the 'Beaters' and dogs would work their way towards them in a line, whooping, hollering and wielding big sticks, as they tried to coax any birds nestling there up into the air.

Our first few runs were largely uneventful with barely a shot being fired, but it was still pleasant enough to wander between different sites, sipping all manner of concoctions from various hip flasks.

We hadn't managed to bag many birds to date but soon stumbled on an area where the pheasants seemed to have gathered in greater numbers. I hadn't seen a single bird all day but as I bashed my way through the undergrowth, I could see a large male pecking at the ground a few feet in front of me. There were no other beaters or dogs near me at the time and I decided that this would indeed be 'my bird.' I ran towards it, crashing through the scrub, waving my arms about and making as much noise as I could. It certainly had the desired effect. This pheasant wasn't sticking around. He took to the air and flew directly away from me, right into the path of the guns. Perfect.

I shouted 'Forward!' as loudly as I could, watching that handsome plump bird silhouetted against a bright blue sky. A deafening shot rang out just ahead of me, followed by another, as the bird flew on and on into the distance.

I didn't bother to conceal my disappointment and trudged forward yelling 'You useless bastard!' hoping to deride and embarrass the sheer incompetent who had missed such a gilt edged opportunity. I didn't realise the 'Gun' in question was close enough to actually hear what I had said, nor did I realise who it was until I brushed past a couple of shrubs.

Disappointment was etched across his face, his still smoking gun cradled in his arms.

'Bad luck Iva,' I said. 'Perhaps we'll get him next year.'

It was probably just as well he had fired off both cartridges.

I had to leave the shoot a bit early, not for fear of Iva's retribution but because I wanted to put the finishing touches to a presentation I was scheduled to make the next day.

A contact I had made through a local business networking group had asked me to take part in an 'Introduction to Business' workshop at a nearby secondary school.

My task was to make a short presentation to groups of fifteen year old schoolgirls, outlining the structure of Jim's Mowing and what exactly constitutes a franchise.

I prepared a PowerPoint presentation that explained the company's origins and ethos, before detailing its system of fees, territory and work allocation.

The first group was herded into a classroom at 10.00am and soon after they were introduced to all things Jim's Mowing.

Twenty minutes and not a single question later they were ushered out again, with the exception of one girl who had incurred the wrath of her teacher. I didn't know what she had done but she was clearly in serious trouble. After much finger wagging and gnashing of teeth, the teacher directed the child towards me, demanding she apologise.

I had no idea what had occurred and felt quite embarrassed for her. As far as I could recall no one had misbehaved during the presentation and it's not as if I was struck by any flying objects throughout.

'I'm really sorry,' she said sheepishly, her chin resting against her chest. 'I'm just really tired.'

I looked up at the clock on the wall. It was twenty past ten.

'That's alright,' I said. 'Don't worry about it,' then laughing, I added 'You didn't fall asleep did you?'

'Yes,' she said.

I was crushed.

I didn't expect to be mobbed afterwards, much less signing autographs, but how more boring could my presentation have been? In just twenty minutes I had transformed a bright, intelligent, healthy adolescent into a narcoleptic.

I shuffled into the staff room and slouched on a couch in the company of some of the other presenters. I confessed my crime, together with the fact that I now just wanted to go home and was thereafter coached and cajoled by some bloke from Euro Tunnel. He assured me that these were indeed very bright and clever kids and that they would not respond to simply being lectured to. What I needed to do to was give them a task, a project they could work through that might stimulate their minds.

Emboldened, I returned to the fray and gave the next group the task of developing an advertising concept that we might use as a poster or press ad to recruit new franchisees.

I divided the class into groups of four and gave them each ten minutes to develop and sketch an idea.

The results were outstanding. Some groups developed ideas that contrasted city landscapes with urban greenery and outcomes that promised a more attractive lifestyle. One idea was even better than the recruitment concept we ourselves had developed and were currently using. Our concept pictured a Jim's Mowing franchisee sitting on a ride on mower, beneath a headline that read 'How do you commute to work?' The concept that emanated from Tonbridge Girls Grammar, showed a group of unhappy, frustrated commuters sitting on a train, seemingly unaware that behind them (through the windows of the train), we could see the lifestyle opportunity a Jim's Mowing franchise represents. Franchisees could be seen mowing lawns, pruning shrubs and trimming hedges. The sky was blue, the grass was green and the sun was shining. What's more, the picture of the unhappy commuters in the foreground would appear in black and white. Above it all a headline read 'Where would you rather be?'

I thought it was absolutely brilliant, as clever and thoughtful a concept as the most experienced creative team in a top flight London ad agency would have come up with. At the time, Beth, Izzy, Katie and Louisa were fifteen year old schoolgirls. I am predicting a bright future for them all.

CHAPTER 29

EXIT STRATEGY

Relationships and business partnerships can be difficult to maintain at the best of times and ours was certainly no different.

My business partner and I had been thrust together when Jason returned to Australia more out of necessity than through any careful planning or consideration. In hindsight it was destined never to work. Our entire operation was based in Kent, whilst he lived in Norfolk. Geographically it was impossible for each of us to contribute anything like an equal amount of time and effort. There were other factors that were holding us back as well. We didn't have a sufficient amount of working capital from the outset (which in plain English means not enough money) and despite our best efforts, we hadn't managed to recruit a sufficient number of franchisees to sustain and build the business to the degree we had hoped. I think cultural differences contributed to that equation as well but to my mind, the exercise was never properly implemented from the outset. Notwithstanding the fact some of our franchisees had made a tremendous success of their businesses, too many others had failed and surrendered their initial investment, citing a lack of support and overall growth.

It is easy to dismiss failures as 'just something that happens' but the fact is I don't believe we held up our end of the deal to the degree that we should and that those who invested in us and in the Jim's Mowing brand were right to expect. It wasn't through a lack of effort or desire but insufficient means. I simply couldn't afford to work six or seven days in the business, travelling the length and breadth of the country while continuing to borrow more and more money to prop it up. It was difficult enough not to draw an income but the stress of an ever increasing debt was weighing heavily on me and above all, it was affecting the support I was able to provide our franchisees.

I still had the greatest faith in Jim's Mowing and believed it could go on to be a great success in the UK. My problem was simply sustaining myself and the business in the ensuing two or three years before it did. That combined with the fact we had (I believe) made some fundamental errors in how we packaged the whole opportunity. I still remember how sick I felt when I first looked over Greg Puzzolo's shoulder at the purpose built VW Transporter on his computer screen. Yes there was much more traffic in the UK and narrower streets but Jim's Mowing had been built off the back of thousands of cheap trailers that could be towed behind a vehicle that a franchisee already owned. The vehicles we developed to use in the UK, for all their practicality and distinctive marketing effectiveness were simply too expensive.

I decided the best approach for all concerned would be for me to sell my stake in the business to an investor who had the capacity to take the business forward. Thereafter perhaps the company could employ someone to manage its day to day operation (as I had done) and over time build its network of regional franchisors, which is without doubt the key to providing franchisees with a proper level of support.

We had been resident in the Lakeview Stables office for three years. A period that had simply flown by and it made little sense to extend the lease for any significant period if I wasn't going to be around for much longer.

My partner proposed we move the operation to Norfolk. I disagreed but after an exchange of emails that secured Jason's support (he was still a minor shareholder), I was 'converted.' To be fair though, it made sense. It was easier for me to move and given he had found a suitable office not far from where he lived it would give him the opportunity to spend more time in the office. The most significant down side however was the fact we would be unable to accommodate two very loyal and hard working employees in Cathy and Roma.

A few months later we were ensconced at Ketteringham Hall, a once stately home south west of Norwich that had been converted into offices. Roma and I were commuting from Kent and staying two nights a week in Norfolk, while Cathy managed to secure a new job not far from where we originally were.

I was still a great believer in the Jim's system and despite some of the difficulties we had encountered, I could see all sorts of opportunity in the UK.

I had kept Jim informed of my plans and expressed an interest in developing a new division in the UK myself. I had seen and met a few Jim's Test and Tag people at the conference and thought there was tremendous potential for the business in the UK. Jim had granted the rights to a couple of blokes who were making a great success of things in Australia and suggested that I get in touch. After a few emails and phone calls, I was convinced I would have the right business partners and with all the experience and knowledge I had gained from my Jim's Mowing venture, I felt sure that together, we could make a good fist of it.

The whole idea however was entirely contingent upon me selling my stake in the mowing business, as I would have neither the time nor the money otherwise.

For the time being, we were obliged to answer phone calls and allocate job leads to our franchisees and to help us we employed a recent school leaver for a couple of months before she enrolled in university at Sheffield.

Sophie was tall, blonde and athletic. She was eighteen and seemed to think that hiding behind the fridge and suddenly leaping out at people (all but instigating a massive heart seizure), was an excellent way to pass the time on the odd slow afternoon.

I was probably lucky to survive that day at all, as I was later called upon to demonstrate how our battery operated 'fly zapping tennis racquet' worked.

It's quite simple' I said, demonstrating my forehand. 'You just push the button here and whack the little beast like so' tapping the head of the racquet against the ball of my thumb as I did.

'Why doesn't that hurt your hand?' she asked.

'Well it's got these wires running across it,' I said, pointing with my finger. 'The fly itself slips through...'

There is a sticker attached to the racquet that reads 'This is not a toy.' I wish it was bigger. I might have noticed it. I might have read it and I might even have paid attention to it. Lest anyone be in any doubt, two AA batteries connected to a wire mesh (designed to electrocute small insects), can still pack one hell of a punch. At least they do when you stick the tip of your index finger in there.

I continued to commute from Kent until the end of the cricket season and given the sale of my stake was likely to take some time to facilitate, I rented a flat on the outskirts of a town called Wymondham. By now winter was setting in and I was watching an unhealthy amount of television.

We managed to enlist two new franchisees in December and one of our incumbents secured regional rights for much of Buckinghamshire at the same time. With a few other sales in the mix for the New Year our financial situation would improve but I was determined to move on.

The overriding factor surrounding my departure was who would be responsible for supporting and communicating with our franchise network. Many of our people had said they had bought into 'me' as much as the system, which made the exit process all the more difficult to justify.

One of our most successful, energetic and ambitious franchisees lived and worked in King's Lynn, not all that far from the new office. Andy Johnson used to work as a printer and in the two years he had been operating a franchise he had built a good base of customers, taken on an employee and expressed an interest in securing the rights to a region. I thought Andy would be an ideal person to take over my role. He had all the attributes we were looking for. He was experienced, friendly and given he had made a great success of his own venture, credible.

Andy would need to find someone to manage his own franchise and given he had regional aspirations, I thought we could structure a deal whereby he could secure the rights he was after as a kind of 'part salary arrangement' for a couple of years.

He was happy with the idea and I thought it made perfect sense. All I needed now was a buyer.

CHAPTER30

THE LAST CHAPTER

I don't think I will ever forget the day I was driving south from Norwich on the M11, when the phone rang.

We had (at my business partner's insistence) relocated our office to Norfolk and I was making my way south to Kent for a weekend of cricket.

I pulled over and spoke to a fellow who was effectively Jim Penman's number two and at the time the head of the Jim's Mowing Division.

He had visited the UK a couple of weeks before and attended a conference of franchisees that we had hastily organised to coincide with his visit. As it turned out his primary purpose was to investigate the many complaints and allegations that numerous franchisees had made against my business partner.

In short, he told me that he had submitted a report upon his return to Melbourne and that Jim had subsequently decided to terminate the UK Master

Franchise Agreement and restructure the entire business.

'Don't worry' he said, 'you have got nothing to worry about.'

Apparently there was a clause in our contract with Jim's Group that gave franchisees the opportunity to effectively vote the UK management out of office, once a thorough investigation of complaints and grievances had been undertaken.

In order to comply, Jim's number two would conduct a series of conference call interviews with all the parties involved and thereafter decide upon an appropriate course of action.

The decision had of course already been made and the entire exercise that followed was little more than a charade.

I agreed to co-operate for three reasons. Firstly, I felt I had no choice, secondly I felt a tremendous responsibility to the forty or so franchisees we had already recruited and thirdly because of the rock solid personal assurances I had been given with regard to my own role going forward.

If they gave out medals for naivety, I reckon I would have a drawer full.

Early one morning (soon after the process had been enacted), there was a knock at the door of my flat. I opened it to see my (now former) business partner standing with a security guard. He handed me an envelope, said 'I'm sorry but you leave me no choice' and left.

The envelope contained a letter. Apparently I was guilty of gross misconduct. My employment and directorship had been terminated with immediate effect, just as the car I had been driving was being towed away.

What's more, my computer had been impounded, the office locks changed and any attempt to enter the building would be considered an act of trespass.

Soon after, our web site announced that the company was engaged in commercial litigation with Jim's Group in Australia and that we were effectively no longer trading.

It was a lot to take in and about to get much worse.

The following day another envelope was delivered. By contrast, this one was about two inches thick. It contained copies of emails, letters and personal correspondence dating back several months, together with a solicitor's letter and legal documents alerting me to the fact I was being sued in the UK High Court. The alleged offence was 'Conspiracy to Defraud' and it was accompanied by a financial damages claim in the order of five million pounds, which at the time was in excess of ten million dollars Australian.

That evening, I picked up the phone and called Jim's Group in Melbourne, asking to speak to the head of the Mowing Division, only to discover that he had resigned the previous day and left without trace, so I asked to speak with Jim.

I explained that despite the many promises and assurances his number two had given me some weeks before, nothing of the sort had eventuated. Quite the opposite in fact.

'I am not going to honour vague undertakings made by

other people' he said.

I was shocked and rendered almost speechless, but went on to explain (as calmly and succinctly as I could), that my former business partner wasn't just suing Jim's Group over the contract termination but me as well, with an entirely separate action, alleging I had orchestrated the entire exercise for my own benefit.

I had done exactly what I had been asked to do and sought only to protect the interests of the many UK franchisees who had invested their money and faith in the Jim's concept.

'That's your problem' he replied.

Over the next few days I managed to divert any incoming calls to my mobile. That way I could still allocate any job leads to franchisees, while I recorded the details on the Jim's system via the internet at the Wyndonham library.

Over the course of the next twelve months, I enlisted the services of a solicitor and successfully defended the High Court action, before returning some months later to the very same court, presided over by the very same judge, after an appeal was lodged.

Despite the enormous personal and financial strain, I delighted in the judge's closing remarks, as he stared down the protagonist and his legal team, when dismissing the appeal.

'I am quite sure that Mr. Harrison is sick of this' he said 'and so am I!'

He was right.

Soon after, I severed all ties with Jim's Group and returned to Australia, from where I successfully defended a third UK High Court legal action and set about creating an exciting and rewarding future.

It is one that I hope allows me to return (one day) to England, as I long to visit some of the wonderful cricket grounds in Kent and Sussex where I played and umpired. I hope to play again with Shipbourne, meet up with my many friends and watch a game on Sevenoaks Vine with a pint of real ale in my hand.

How hard could it be?

Printed by Amazon Italia Logistica S.r.l.
Torrazza Piemonte (TO), Italy

10715596R00141